Morning Meetings & Closing Circles

Classroom-Ready Activities That Increase Student Engagement and Create a Positive Learning Community

Monica Dunbar

ULYSSES PRESS

Published in the United States by:
Ulysses Press
P. O. Box 3440
Berkeley, CA 94703
www.ulyssespress.com

ISBN: 978-1-64604-067-4
Library of Congress Control Number: 2020935668

Printed in the United States by Kingery Printing Company
10 9 8 7 6 5 4 3 2 1

Acquisitions editor: Claire Sielaff
Managing editor: Claire Chun
Project editor: Renee Rutledge
Editor: Debra Riegert
Proofreader: Kate St. Clair
Cover design: what!design @ whatweb.com
Cover art: shutterstock.com—large circles © Derek Brumby; small circle © Rudchenko Liliia; background texture © Borja Andreu
Interior design: Jake Flaherty

Contents

Chapter 5
Starting Your First Closing Circle 125

Introduction

Welcome to the wonderful world of morning meetings and closing circles! I am so happy you are here. Are you new to these procedures? No problem! You have come to the right place. We are going to get you up and running in no time at all, and with very little effort and preparation on your part. Are you more experienced with morning meetings and closing circles? That's great, too, because the ideas presented in this book will help rejuvenate and reenergize your meeting and circle routines.

My love for morning meetings and closing circles began in my fifteenth year of teaching. While browsing the Internet one day, I came across two daily routines that teachers around the globe were implementing in their classrooms. Teachers in elementary and high school classrooms were hosting little get-togethers with their students, at the beginning and end of each day. I thought it was a wonderful idea until I began to do more research on the topic. Different authors presented different ideas on how meetings and circles should take place, and I was worried that I was going to do something that was ineffective and contrary to what I wanted to accomplish. To say I was overwhelmed by the wealth of opinions and ideas on these topics was an understatement.

Although I loved the idea of morning meeting and closing circles, I did not have a lot of spare time to sift through the many books, articles, and opinions on how to host these classroom get-togethers. I found myself liking aspects of some books but not others and found ideas around the Internet that fit my personality and teaching philosophy. With all these new ideas floating around in my head from many different perspectives,

I sat down and came up with a morning meeting and closing circle formula that works best for me and my students. That is the formula I am sharing with you in this book.

Feeling a little overwhelmed yourself? Let me comfort you. Repeat after me: "There is no right or wrong way to host a morning meeting or closing circle." The ideas provided in this book are just guidelines to get you started or to give you a little extra support. You know your students and teaching style better than anyone else. Part of the magic of these procedures is adding your own special twist to how you host a meeting or a circle. Trust me, your students are going to learn so much about you and themselves because of what you bring to the morning meeting and closing circle experience. I guarantee that these activities will not only become the highlight of your students' day, but your day as well!

The topics in this book will provide you with the opportunity to get to know your students on a deeper level and to add an element of social emotional learning to the school day. These 100 activities will not only ensure that you and your students are practicing a wide variety of social, emotional, educational, and physical activities, but will also serve as a guide to challenge you, the teacher, to implement your own morning meetings and closing circles once the book is finished. The relationships you forge with your students during the first fifty activities will shape the way you continue the morning meeting and closing circle process for the rest of the school year.

So, without further ado, let's jump into the wonderful world of morning meetings and closing circles. With just 20 dedicated minutes a day, you will foster a greater sense of community, collaboration, and mutual respect within your classroom and among your students. I also guarantee you will all have a great time participating in these activities!

Chapter 1
What Are Morning Meetings?

Think of yourself for a moment. When you enter your school first thing in the morning, what is it that you do? Do you dive directly into your work? Do you tackle a pile of corrections on top of your desk right away? Probably not! If you are like me, you say good morning to your co-workers, empty your personal mailbox, engage in conversations, talk about the day ahead, and perhaps you even grab a cup of coffee. Essentially, you are easing yourself into your new work day.

Now think of your students. For various reasons, your students might not come to school ready to take on the day. Some may not have slept well the night before. Some might have had a bad experience, perhaps at home or on the school bus, that has made them feel insecure and vulnerable. Some may be ill and others may be hungry. On the other hand, some may be superexcited about the day ahead. We never know what reality our students are living. It is impossible to know for certain what they are going through on any particular day or at any particular moment. Does it seem reasonable to ask our students to get straight to work the moment they enter the classroom, considering we, as adults, do not?

To facilitate the transition from child to learner at the beginning of each school day requires a metaphorical bridge; one that helps children embrace, with pride, the title of student. According to a study published in the *Journal of Applied Behavior Analysis*, the way in which a teacher greets their students every morning has a direct effect on the increase of on-task academic activity.[1] Morning meetings are designed to enhance and build upon this daily greeting. Taking a few precious minutes at the beginning of the school day to come together as a community, allows children to relax, compose themselves, and build upon their confidence before beginning a day of academics.

Quite simply, morning meetings are mini-classroom assemblies that are held at the beginning of each school day. To an outside observer, a well-run morning meeting will look similar to circle time routines that are

---

1   Allan Allday and Kerri Pakurar, "Effects of Teacher Greetings on Student On-Task Behavior." *Journal of Applied Behavior Analysis* 40, no. 2 (2007): 317–20, https://doi.org/10.1901/jaba.2007.86-06.

popular in preschool and kindergarten. Circle times in the lower grades are mainly used to talk about the calendar, the weather, and academics like counting or recognizing colors. Morning meetings are an expansion of this idea. In the elementary and high school grades, morning meetings are a special learning experience, dedicated to the development of verbal communication, active listening, and mutual respect among all participants. This special time, with emphasis placed on the simple art of communicating and active listening, provides students with the opportunity to develop these skills in a safe, teacher-guided, social setting.

The benefits of hosting morning meetings are abundant. Students learn patience, kindness, and how to deal with and accept randomness. They learn to listen to others and truly hear what others are saying to them. They learn to take risks and step outside of their comfort zones. They learn to talk and cooperate with others they might never have chosen to talk to on their own. They learn to deal with their feelings of being shy and anxious. They learn self-control and most importantly, they learn that they have a voice that is to be heard, respected, and valued.

The greatest benefit of the morning meeting routine is that students learn strategies for social, emotional, and behavioral learning through talking, observation, and practice. Textbooks, workbooks, and curriculum are set aside during these meetings and students learn subtle social cues from listening to and watching their teacher. As the morning meeting routine develops throughout the school year, the teacher and students learn to speak openly with one another, talk respectfully to one another, and forge a relationship built on trust and mutual respect. The skills learned in each morning meeting are continually reinforced throughout the year, which ensures that all the positivity students are practicing become second nature.

A sense of belonging is a basic human need, just like the need for food and shelter.[2] Students who feel loved and accepted in a classroom setting

---

2   Karyn Hall, "Create a Sense of Belonging: Finding Ways to Belong Can Ease the Pain of Loneliness," *Psychology Today,* March 24, 2014, https://www.psychologytoday.com/us/blog/pieces-mind/201403/create-sense-belonging.

will perform better academically and behaviorally. This is my favorite outcome of the morning meeting experience.

Watching the sense of community flourish among the students in my classroom was pure joy. As my students began to implement the social skills worked on during our morning meeting time together, I noticed that they were getting along better, and their collective classroom behavior changed for the better as well. My students were more attentive and happier, and the level of engagement in their classwork was off the charts.

Coincidence? Maybe, but I doubt it. Once students feel a personal connection to you and their classmates, the more emotionally invested they'll be in their education. Positivity promotes positivity, and morning meetings are the perfect way to start each day on the right foot.

Increasing student engagement is the key to unlocking educational success. The problem that teachers face is that they are working with children with many different academic, social, and emotional needs. A lot of students follow individualized education plans as well. Not only do teachers struggle to fit in all the academic requirements their students need, they now have to plan how to meet the social, emotional, and behavioral needs of their students as well. How can one teacher to do that without knowing the background of their students? How can a teacher know which characteristics to focus on? How can a teacher build a trusting relationship with their students without making the students feel uncomfortable? All the answers lie within the first 10 minutes of each day.

By focusing on all the other needs of our students before their academic needs, we show students that we care about them and are genuinely interested in their health and well-being. Once a student feels that level of love and caring, behavior and academic improvement increase. The students begin to become active participants in their learning. The teacher-student dynamic changes from teacher centered to community centered. And that is when real learning can start to take place.

If you think students are the only ones who benefit from morning meetings, think again! As an educator, you will learn a wealth of priceless information about your students. You will learn about their hopes and dreams, their likes and dislikes, and you will gain valuable information about their home lives. You will laugh with your students. You will celebrate their achievements. The social and emotional development of your students from the beginning of the year to the end will amaze you as you continue to develop strong relationships with each and every one of them.

Beginning a morning meeting routine may seem a little strange to you and your students. It takes time for the rhythm of the meetings to become familiar and comfortable. Some students may be too shy to participate right away while others may try to monopolize the sharing experience. Some students may be in the midst of learning English as a second language and may feel too self-conscious to speak in front of their classmates. Some children may have a hard time sitting patiently while waiting for their turn. All of these are okay! With your gentle guidance, all of your students can and will actively participate in all the wonderful, well-structured morning meeting activities provided in this book. And when that happens, you will be able to sit back and watch the magic happening in your classroom throughout the entire school day.

Chapter 2

What Are Closing Circles?

The end of the school day can be a struggle for both students and teachers. Packing up school bags, arranging the classroom, getting dressed, and heading out to the school bus or pick-up area is very hectic! Plus, students are tired after a full day of learning. How many times have you felt like the last period of the day would never end? Have you ever felt stressed and rushed trying to get everyone ready to leave at the end of the day? Have you ever breathed a sigh of relief once you have everyone out the door? I used to feel that way all the time.

To make matters worse, I began leaving work feeling relieved to have survived the end-of-the-day madness. I returned home each night to my family who commented on how I was becoming more and more irritable with each passing work day. How negative is that? Why wasn't I feeling triumphant over all the wonderful things my students and I accomplished? I knew that I had to do something to flip the narrative; to force myself to end each day on a more positive note. Once again, I took to the Internet to find some inspiration and that search led me to closing circles.

As important as morning meetings are to the beginning of the day, closing circles are just as significant. Run in much the same way as their morning counterpart, closing circles are another way to reinforce concepts learned throughout the day and to continue to practice important interpersonal skills.

Coming together at the end of the school day brings a sense of closure to you and your students and gives everyone the opportunity to decompress and reflect upon their day. The closing circle provides students and teachers an opportunity to speak and listen to one another in a safe atmosphere and allows them both to be heard and offer their own perspectives.[3]

The benefits of closing circles are numerous. Whether students had a good day or a tough day, a closing circle can help build trust and cooperation in the classroom. This safe environment enables students to

---

3   K. Pranis, *The Little Book of Circle Processes* (Intercourse, PA: Good Books, 2005).

take risks so that they can do their best learning.[4] Did you notice that a student was frustrated at some point during the day? Closing circle time would be a great time to discuss feelings of frustration and how to deal with them in a positive manner. Did you have difficulty with a student during the day? Flipping the narrative during a closing circle and concentrating on the positive qualities of that particular student will do so much more for the child's self-esteem than getting upset at them. Bringing up an issue during a closing circle, a place that students will learn to feel safe, strengthens the relationship you have, or would like to have, with that child.

The closing circle times I have shared with my students have been a wonderful addition to my daily routine. It feels so good being able to leave the school knowing that my students and I are leaving each other on a positive note. As the school year's closing circles progressed, students would ask me if it was circle time yet! If that doesn't show you how much the students looked forward to and loved closing circle time, then I don't know what would!

Another thing that is great about the closing circle process is that it starts around the time when students are starting to reach their breaking point. Be realistic. Are all your students fully engaged right to the last bell of the day? I know mine aren't. This is the time when students exhibit behaviors that are less than satisfactory. That is another reason why closing circles play such an important part in your daily routine. It gives you and your students a chance to break away from formal curriculum and academic activities and ease into a more social and emotional frame of mind before leaving for the day.

The goal of closing circles is simple. You want to wrap up the school day in the best possible way. You want to allow you and your students an opportunity to reflect upon the events of the day. Whether you would like to review concepts taught during the day, discuss issues that came up between students, or even sing a song, this time is set up to finish the

4   Dana Januszka and Kristen Vincent, *Closing Circles: 50 Activities for Ending the Day in a Positive Way* (Turners Falls, MA: Northeast Foundation for Children, Inc., 2012).

day on a positive note. You and your students will still be exhausted from all the engaging activities and academic rigor of the day, but you will all go home with peace in your hearts and calm in your minds.

Some of you may be worried about the amount of time it takes to host a closing circle. My first few weeks of closing circles took between 15 and 20 minutes to complete. Don't worry about it! It takes time for you and your students to adjust to this new routine. In addition, especially if you are beginning this routine at the start of a new school year, you will have many students who are shy and not yet comfortable to share with you and their classmates. Just like the morning meetings, it will take time for you and your students to get into a rhythm where the process feels familiar and natural. That is normal. Once you get your timing down pat, you will be able to have your closing circle completed in just 10 minutes or less! My advice to you is to be consistent and precise! Make sure your students understand and follow the rules you have set for the closing meeting procedures. As time goes by, your students will become familiar with the process and the routines will become automatic for everyone!

Chapter 3

How Do I Start a Morning Meeting and Closing Circle Routine?

When planning to begin your morning meeting or closing circle routine, there are four main factors that you need to consider before starting. The following is a checklist to help you out:

1. How many students do I have?

Morning meetings and closing circles are successful with small or large groups of students, however, many morning meetings require partner or group work. Because of time restraints, such as specialist teachers coming in for first period classes or special events that may be taking place, it is very important to know how you can quickly group your students for various activities. The activities provided in this book mostly suggest grouping your students into groups of even numbers of two or four. With that being said, you also have to be willing to jump in and take the spot of someone if you have an odd number of students or if a student is absent for the day.

2. How much room do I have?

Depending on how much room you have to move around, you might need to get creative with how you host your morning meetings. Ideally, morning meetings and closing circles are done in a circle formation but classroom sizes and the number of students can make that idea unrealistic. I have had successful morning meetings take place with as little as 18 students and as many as 28. Take an inventory of the amount of free space you have to dedicate to morning meetings in your classroom. Do you have room for your entire class to sit in a circle? Will you have them sit on the floor? On a carpet? On chairs? If you find that you do not have enough space, do not despair! You can always host a morning meeting while the students are sitting at (or on!) their desks. With the group of 28, there was no room with all the desks and furniture to make a circle without having to move all the desks each morning. Instead, I opted for the students to remain at their desks during the morning meeting. The students will benefit from the morning meeting experience no matter where they are situated.

3. Am I willing to devote up to 20 minutes a day to develop these routines in my classroom?

Those unfamiliar with the benefits of morning meeting and closing circles will probably shudder at the thought of having to "give up" 20 minutes of teaching time in order to host and facilitate these daily routines. Don't worry about it! Realistically, your students need these precious minutes to get them ready to face the day at the beginning and to decompress at the end. Consider this time as an investment in the well-being of your students and an investment in your classroom management plan! Would you rather your students be engaged in meaningful conversations with their peers, or in off-task or avoidance work behaviors?

If 20 minutes a day seems unrealistic to you because of administrative or timetable restrictions, I strongly suggest just starting with the morning meetings. We want our students beginning their academic day with a positive attitude toward you and their schoolwork. Keep in mind that as your students learn to effectively communicate with each other and learn how to truly listen to what each other is saying, you will see that those skills transfer into every aspect of your classroom. My advice is to jump into morning meetings and closing circles with both feet. As you will learn from this book, the best way to increase student engagement and promote a positive learning environment is by doing both the morning meeting and closing circle on a daily basis. Trust me, the more time you dedicate time to these routines, the sooner you will notice a change for the better in your students.

4. Am I willing to stick with it?

The key to running effective and successful morning meetings and closing circles is consistency. It requires daily repetition in order to reinforce all the routines and goals that you want to instill in your students. There will be days, especially in the beginning, where it will feel like the process is not working. You may want to skip a day, but it is important to keep up the routine. Like any lesson plan, some morning meetings and closing circles will not run as smoothly as you hoped, but you must not allow those 10 or 20 minutes to get you down. Push yourself through those hard days and continue working the routines with your students. Deciding to partake in morning meetings and closing circles in order to benefit from all the positives of the experiences requires you to make a long-term commitment to hosting them. For these to work, and for your students to benefit from all the social, emotional, and developmental learning that will take place, you have no choice but to be all in.

Now that you have decided to go ahead with morning meetings and/ or closing circles, you can let the fun begin! Get ready to watch your students shine and participate like they never have before. In a very short period of time, you will fall in love with these routines and all that they have to offer. Don't even think about forgetting or choosing not to do one! Your students, who will love these routines just as much as you, will definitely remind you when it is time to have one.

There are no right or wrong ways to host a morning meeting or closing circle. Develop your own procedure that works well for you, fits into your daily school schedule, and is not overwhelming to integrate into your daily routine. The morning meetings and closing circles are designed to enhance your interpersonal relationships with your students and are not meant to be added pressure to your already busy day. You need them to work for you in order for them to work for your students.

Morning Meetings and Closing Circles While Social Distancing

In our rapidly changing world, educators have had to navigate new teaching methods that include virtual learning and social distancing. Many of you might be wondering how you can successfully implement the morning meetings and closing circle activities that are presented in this book. The answer lies in your ability as a teacher to think on your feet, your ability to adapt to numerous challenges, and your creativity. But don't worry! You've got this!

For those of you mandated to teach virtually, the inability to have proximity with your students will change how you do your morning meetings and closing circles, but that should not deter you from giving them a try. Your discussion and rules will reflect the distance learning rules and expectations that you will need to establish with your students. Your morning meetings will focus on speaking and social skills more so than physical activities. Therefore, you will be fostering more personal and interpersonal connections with the students through speaking and listening to one another.

Those of you who will be working in a classroom setting may have to follow new directives for social distancing in your classroom. What those directives are depends on where you live and the school district you work for. Should your students be placed in small groups called pods, or bubbles, these students will be working in close proximity to each other and, therefore, can participate in all the activities together in their respective groups. Please ensure that you and the students have access to personal protective equipment such as face masks or shields, and that students have access to hand sanitizer or soap and hot water in order to wash their hands before and after each activity.

Those of you who will be in the classroom but must have their students respect the 6-feet-apart distance rule can have your students participate in most of the morning meetings and closing circles from their own desks. As with virtual learning, you will have to adapt many of these activities as they are presented in this book, but please do not underestimate the power of promoting and practicing speaking and active listening skills.

At any time you or any of your students feel uncomfortable attempting any of the morning meetings and closing circles because of physical proximity, please take a step back and rethink how you could do the activity from a safer distance. Your health and safety, as well as the health and safety of your students, is paramount. These activities are meant to bring out the best in all of you, not to add any undue stress or anxiety. Just keep reminding yourself that there is no right or wrong way to conduct one of these meetings. No matter how you choose to perform these activities, you and your students are going to benefit greatly from the effort you put in to making them a success.

Chapter 4
Starting Your First Morning Meeting

The goal of this chapter is to help you get your very first morning meeting up and running.

Establish Randomness Using Craft Sticks with Students' Names on Them

As outlined below, randomness is a difficult concept for students to accept, but it is a necessity when it comes to morning meetings. Choosing sticks to make groups or to choose speakers is a strategy that comes with the following benefits:

- It alleviates students from raising their hands each time they have something to contribute to the discussion.

- Picking sticks challenges students to learn to wait their turn when communicating within group of people.

- Randomness teaches students that although they may have something to say, they might not be given the opportunity to do so.

- Picking sticks to form groups provides students the opportunity to work with students with whom they might not choose to work with.

- No student has to feel like they are unwanted or unaccepted when the class is asked to form groups on their own.

- Picking sticks allows for teachers to choose a wide variety of students to contribute to the class discussion. It gives every child in the class an equal opportunity to take part in the morning meeting experience.

Your craft sticks do not need to be fancy. I use regular brown craft sticks and write the names of my students on them with black marker. I keep them in a little mason jar that travels with me throughout the school day. I love the idea of randomness so much that I use the strategy in my math and language arts classes as well! My students have transferred our usage of the sticks to their other classes and it has been a wonderful classroom management tool. My students wait patiently for their names to be called when we are reading or correcting, and I do not have the same confident students raising their hands all the time to answer questions.

Choose a Starting Signal

Having a starting signal is a great way for your students to know when it is time to practice their morning meeting skills, conversational skills, or sharing time. Your start signal could be a simple "Go!" command to let the students know they can begin their activity. Other great ways to give a starting signal is to use a Bluetooth wireless doorbell, sound buzzers, or a handclapping sequence. Whatever you choose to use, make sure to be consistent. You will be training your students to respond appropriately to whatever sound you choose. Hearing your specific starting signal lets your students know that it is time to get to work on their morning meeting skills.

Introduce the Morning Meeting Concept to Your Class

Your students might not know what morning meetings are so this is your time to explain everything. Let them know that this is a new classroom routine that will take place every morning. Explain to them how it will run and that you will be all having a great amount of fun together. It is also important to let them know that once the class is comfortable with the routine, it will only take 10 minutes out of each morning to execute. This part is very important as it teaches children to be on task, respect time limits, and manage their time wisely during meeting time.

Call the Morning Meeting to Order

When you are ready to begin, you must call your meeting to order. Every time your students hear you call the morning meeting they should know exactly where to go and what to do. You will have to model for and practice with your students so they will know how to get into the starting formation you want. Have your students practice getting from their seats into formation a few times in order for them to understand how quickly and quietly they need to organize themselves when the meetings are called to order. When it is time to call my meetings to order, I simply state, "Hey, everyone! It's time for our morning meeting!" My students then leave their desks and sit cross-legged on the floor at the front of our classroom. Another requirement I have for my students is that they must sit next to someone different each day.

Greeting

Welcoming everyone into the formation is the best way to start your morning meeting. For the very first meeting, you will need to establish the rules and procedures that you expect your students to respect during morning meeting time. You can set these rules yourself or make it a morning meeting. Because my students are third-graders and usually new to the morning meeting concept, I provide them with the rules I would like for them to follow during our very first meeting together. These include sitting in a circle next to two new people each meeting and respecting the student who has been chosen to talk by listening and not speaking at the same time. While these rules are basic, I do tend to add more as new skills are taught, practiced, and mastered during morning meetings. For example, as students are introduced to the concept of eye contact, I will work that into a new rule for when the students are listening to whomever is speaking.

No matter how you choose to do it, these rules and expectations will become the foundation of your morning meeting routine. Some teachers like to give a rundown of the day ahead and go through the schedule of the day. Others, like myself, enjoy asking my students conversation starter questions to find out how they are feeling or to learn about the activities they did over the weekend. The greeting is a perfect time to have a sing-along for younger students or a recap of current events with older students. No matter what you decide to do, please be consistent, positive, and specific! This greeting may be the first time that day that your students have heard their name said out loud. Please make it count!

Host the Morning Meeting

Here is where you get to set all your planning and preparations into motion! Please feel free to use the 50 morning meetings provided in the next section to begin. They have been prepared to get you up and running with very little preparation time. While you are not obligated to do the morning meetings in the same order as presented in this book, I do suggest that you do, as each meeting is carefully designed to reinforce the structures, concepts, and procedures of the meeting beforehand. Please do not worry about your timing on this first meeting. Take the time to notice the reactions of your students. Notice their smiles and the way they interact with one another. This process is new for everyone involved and it will take time to perfect. As time goes on and your students become more familiar with each other and the morning meeting process, you will undoubtably notice a growing sense of community and respect among everyone in your class.

Adjournment

As with any meeting, bringing it to a complete close is just as important as opening the meeting. You can use this time to get your students back into formation if they have moved around, thank them for their participation, and wish them a great day. This wrap-up should leave you and your students feeling refreshed, energized, and ready to take on the day!

You are all set! I am so excited for you and your students! You are about to embark on a wonderful journey full of mutual respect, conversation, and active listening. You are going to see a positive change in the climate of your classroom and the way in which your students interact with each other. So, what are you waiting for? Your first morning meeting is waiting for you!

1. The Harmony Handshake

Goal: Teach students how to give a handshake. This prepares them to partake in the world of social networking.

Background Knowledge

The meaning and importance of handshaking varies depending on where you live. For North Americans, a handshake can mean many different things. It can be used as a greeting, as a goodbye, and even as a precursor to a business transaction. Today's morning meeting gives students the chance to practice handshaking with their classmates and provides a chance to overcome any uncomfortable feelings related to that gesture.

Procedure

- Model what handshakes look like where you live.
  - Polite grip
  - Polite speed
  - Polite length
  - Retain eye contact

- Model what handshakes should not look like.
  - Too strong of a grip
  - Too fast and too slow
  - Too long or too short
  - No eye contact

- Arrange students into an inner and outer circle. Students in each circle must face each other. When you give your signal to start, have the children practice their handshake with the person in front of them. Once the handshake is finished, have the inner circle rotate one place to the left so that the students are now facing a new handshaking partner. Continue this procedure as many times as you like.

- Ask all students to return to the starting formation. Have a short discussion about how the students felt shaking the hands of their classmates. Challenge the students to shake hands with three other people throughout the school day.

Tips and Tricks

Please be conscious of students with sensory issues or a specific diagnosis that makes touching others or maintaining eye contact difficult. For these students, you can practice a fist bump, a gentle high five, or show them how to place their hands over their hearts when greeting someone. These examples allow your students with sensory issues to participate in the activity while respecting their comfort levels.

Ideas for Your Own Classroom

_____

_____

_____

_____

_____

_____

_____

_____

_____

_____

2. The Staring Contest

Goal: Get students to practice looking others in the eye. This prepares them to partake in social networking.

Background Knowledge

Looking people in the eyes is an important part of greeting others around the world. Just because it is a common practice in many cultures does not mean that it is easy to do. Today's morning meeting moves students out of their comfort zone when it comes to looking people straight in the eyes and gives them an opportunity to break through their discomfort while having a little bit of fun!

Procedure

- Group students into pairs and have them face each other.

- Explain to the students that in most cultures, staring at someone is considered impolite. Today's morning meeting is not to practice staring at people but to practice looking at others directly in their eyes.

- When you give your signal to start, have the students practice looking into the eyes of their partners. It is okay if they blink but they must refrain from speaking to one another. For this first round, have them stare at each other for about 10 seconds.

- For round two, have the students say the alphabet in tandem while staring at each other.

- For round three, have the students continue to stare at each other. For this final round, label the partners as A and B. When it is Partner A's turn, have them verbalize which eye, part of the face, or some other point they think Partner B is focusing on. Most people, when looking into the eyes of someone else, tend to focus on one eye or the other. Some people even focus on the space between the eyes. Continue with partner B.

- Ask all students to return to the starting formation. Pick sticks, as many as you would like, and have those students describe how they felt when staring into the eyes of their partner. Could they tell where their partner was focusing?

Tips and Tricks

Be conscious of students with sensory issues or a specific diagnosis that makes maintaining eye contact difficult. For these students, practice winking with one eye and then the other, or have them stare at an object in the classroom instead of a person. These examples allow your students with sensory issues to participate in the activity while respecting their comfort levels.

Ideas for Your Own Classroom

_____

_____

_____

_____

_____

_____

_____

_____

_____

_____

3. Practice Eye Contact

Goal: Have students practice eye contact in a game situation. Students will continue to practice the use of eye contact in preparation for social networking with others.

Background Knowledge

This activity forces students to pay attention while looking directly in the eyes of their classmates. You can play this game for the duration of the morning meeting or use it as a brain break at any time.

Procedure

- Seat all students in a circle. Make sure there is enough room for children to fall onto their backs without hitting their heads on a wall or piece of furniture.

- Explain that the goal of this game is for the "zoomer" not to get caught by the "detective" as defined below.

- Pick one craft stick and name the student. This person will be the "detective" and will wait outside the classroom until you say it is time to return.

- While the "detective" is outside of the classroom, pick another craft stick. This student will be the "zoomer."

- Ask the "detective" to come back into the circle. Tell the "zoomer" to widen their eyes at their classmates around the circle, with the exception of the "detective." Once the "zoomer" makes eye contact and widens their eyes to a classmate, that classmate carefully falls backward and stays that way until the end of the game.

- Give the "detective" three chances to guess the "zoomer."

Tips and Tricks

For this game to work well, make sure that the students in the circle make eye contact with several people during the game, not only with the "zoomer." It is also important that the "zoomer" keeps track of where the "detective" is looking so that he or she does not get caught.

Ideas for Your Own Classroom

_____

_____

_____

_____

_____

_____

_____

_____

_____

_____

_____

_____

_____

_____

_____

_____

4. Three Minutes of Silence

Goal: Teach students to practice listening attentively to the sounds around them. Students will practice using their sense of hearing to be able to listen attentively when having a social conversation with others.

Background Knowledge

One of the best ways to enhance one sense is to block out the others. Today your students will close their eyes and rest quietly for three minutes. These three minutes will provide students with an opportunity to put all their energy and attention into hearing what is going on around them without visual distractions. This will seem very long but it is important for the students to take the time to truly listen to all the sounds around them. As students learn to converse with others, the ability for them to listen critically and attentively, while blocking out other stimuli, will become more and more important.

Procedure

- Have the students arrange themselves somewhere in the classroom in a comfortable position so that they do not move or distract others.

- Tell the students that for this activity they will be completely still and silent for three minutes and that they must have their eyes closed for the entire time.

- Before giving the starting signal, instruct the students to listen as closely as they can to all of the different sounds they hear during the three minutes of silence. Have them keep a mental list of what they hear.

- After the three minutes are up, ask your students to return to the starting formation. Have a discussion about all the different sounds they heard during the activity. Was it hard for them to keep their eyes closed? Was it difficult to stay concentrated on listening? What other things did they notice?

To build upon this activity, ask your students to tell you who or what made the sounds that they heard. For example, if a student heard footsteps in the hallway, they may be able to tell you who was walking based on the type of sound, speed, and pressure of the footsteps. Were your classroom windows open during the three minutes of silence? Your students will be able to infer a lot of great information from the sounds coming from outside.

Ideas for Your Own Classroom

_____

_____

_____

_____

_____

_____

_____

_____

_____

_____

_____

_____

_____

5. Listen Up Everyone!

> **Goal:** Teach your students active listening skills.
> Listening attentively to others is a valuable
> component of communication.

Background Knowledge

Students of all ages need to be taught how to actively listen when others are speaking. If students are not able to listen attentively, they will miss important information and may misunderstand important directions. There is a big difference between *hearing* someone talk and *listening* to what they have to say. Today's morning meeting teaches students how to actively listen and gives them a chance to practice this skill.

Procedure

- Model what the different signs of active listening should look like:
  - Maintain eye contact
  - Use appropriate facial expressions
  - Lean slightly toward the speaker
  - Slightly tilt your head to show interest
  - Ask questions when appropriate

- Model what the different signs of active listening should *not* look like:
  - Eyes looking down at the floor or other places
  - Inappropriate facial expressions such as sticking your tongue out or scrunching up your facial muscles
  - Turning your body away from the speaker
  - Showing little or no interest in what the speaker is saying
  - Asking questions that have nothing to with what the speaker is talking about

- Break the students off into pairs. Have them find a place to sit together where they can face each other and talk without being distracted by others.

- When you give the starting signal, have partners take turns talking about their favorite television show. While Partner A is talking, Partner B will practice using the active listening skills. When you sense that the conversations are over, have the partners switch roles and start again.

- Ask all students to return to the starting formation. Pick sticks and ask the students to help you review the signs of active listening.

Tips and Tricks

You can choose to have your students talk about anything during this meeting, but I advise you to choose something familiar. Please note that the actual speaking part may be very difficult for some, especially children in kindergarten to grade 2, as it requires students to speak continuously without much input from the listener. Encourage the students to speak for at least two minutes in order for the listener to practice as many active listening skills as possible.

Ideas for Your Own Classroom

_____

_____

_____

_____

_____

_____

_____

6. Family Matters

Goal: Encourage students to talk about their families with their classmates and practice their active listening skills. The children will be able to practice their conversational and listening skills, which are both important for social networking with others.

Background Knowledge

One of the easiest ways to get students communicating is to have them talk about themselves. For this morning meeting, students will have a conversation with their classmates about their families while continuing to practice their active listening skills.

Procedure

- Review the active listening skills from the previous morning meeting. For example, quickly prompt the students to provide you with examples of good eye contact, appropriate facial expressions, and body language that they remember. This does not need to take more than one minute to do and can be done as a whole circle activity.

- Pick a stick and have that student help you model negative active listening. Have your student talk about what they had for breakfast. While your student is talking, make sure to exaggerate what not to do when actively listening. For example, make it a point to look away from the student talking. Do not maintain eye contact with them. Play with your hair and ask a question that has nothing to do with what your student is talking about. Have the rest of your students point out what you are doing incorrectly.

- With the same student, model what positive active listening should look like. It is important not to over exaggerate during this example because you do not want your students to look unnatural when employing their active listening skills with others.

- Group students into pairs and have them face each other. Have them find a place to sit together where they can face each other and talk, without being distracted.

- Give the start signal. Have partners take turns talking about their families. For example, students can talk about their siblings who are athletes, a brother or sister who has a special musical talent, or even about the jobs that their parents have. While Partner A is talking, Partner B will employ their active listening skills. When you sense that the conversations have completed, have the partners switch roles and start again.

- Ask all students to return to the starting formation. Pick as many sticks as you would like. Should students feel comfortable with talking about their families in front of the class, they may share what their partners have said. If a student does not feel comfortable, it is perfectly fine to allow them to skip their turn.

Tips and Tricks

Although your students are partnered up and interacting with each other, this is an excellent time to learn a lot about their individual families. Walk around the classroom while the students are talking to each other. While you are observing their active listening skills, you will hear students talk candidly about their families. Keep these little bits of information in the back of your mind! You can always use something that you have learned about your students to help grow and strengthen your relationships with them later on.

Ideas for Your Own Classroom

_____

_____

_____

7. Introducing One Another

Goal: Show students how to introduce people to one another.

Background Knowledge

Introducing people takes more than just announcing someone's name to someone else. Today's morning meeting teaches your students how to properly introduce their classmates; a skill that will go far beyond the classroom for many years to come.

Procedure

- Demonstrate the proper steps for introducing someone. Point out to students that they should include the person's name along with "I would like to introduce you to _____."

- Encourage students to include an interesting detail about the person they are introducing such as:

  - "Jeffrey, I would like to introduce you to Kimberly. She is a student from McGill University. Kimberly is studying to become a teacher."

  - "Ms. Smith, I would like for you to meet my sister, Sabrina. She is seven years old and loves to read books from the library."

- Pick a stick and have one student help you model the wrong way to introduce someone. For example, you might say "Class, this is Amanda. She likes to do stuff." Make it very obvious that you are not interested in the person you are introducing.

- With that same student, model what a positive introduction should look like. For example, you might say, "Class, I would like to introduce you to Amanda. She is 8 years old and she rides her bike to school every day. She enjoys reading books and she loves going to her swimming lessons on the weekend." It is important not to overexaggerate during this example because you do not want your students to look unnatural when transferring this lesson outside of the classroom setting.

- Pick sticks to form groups of three students. Have the groups find a place to be together where they can face each other and talk without being distracted by others.

- Give the start signal. Have partners take turns introducing one another. While Partner A is talking, Partners B and C will employ their active listening skills. When you sense that the conversations have completed, have the partners switch roles again until everyone has a chance to practice their introductions.

- Ask all of the students to return to the starting formation next to their partners. Pick as many sticks as you would like. The names of the people you choose will introduce their partners to the class. Those chosen to model can stand or remain in the starting formation.

- Provide a few different social scenario examples that students can use to practice introductions. The social scenarios provided below will give your students an opportunity to role-play various social situations. Make sure students rotate their roles so that they can experience the different facets of introductions.

A. *Student 1*—Him or herself

Student 2—Parent

Student 3—Friend of Student 1

You are at the grocery store with your parent. While doing the grocery shopping, you see a good friend of yours. Use your social skills to greet your friend and then introduce them to your parent.

B. *Student 1*—Him or herself

Student 2—Parent

Student 3—Teacher

It is "Meet the Teacher Night" at school. Use your social skills to introduce your parent to your teacher.

C. *Student 1*—The school's basketball coach

Student 2—Him or herself

Student 3—The basketball coach's child

You are at a fast food restaurant and you notice one of your players waiting in line behind you. Use your social skills to greet your player and introduce them to your child.

D. *Student 1*—Him or herself

Student 2—Manager of the pet shelter

Student 3—Assistant manager of the pet shelter

You would like to volunteer at the local pet shelter. You have been asked to come in for an interview. Use your social skills to introduce yourself to the manager. The manager will then introduce his assistant manager to you.

E. *Student 1*—Him or herself

Student 2—A friend

Student 3—Your friend's parent

You are visiting your friend's house for the first time. When your friend answers the door, greet them appropriately. Then, your friend will use their social skills to introduce you to the parent.

F. *Student 1*—A new student at school

Student 2—Him or herself

Student 3—A friend of student 2

There is a new student at school and you want them to feel welcome. You and your friend decide to greet the student and introduce yourselves, using the social skills you have learned.

G. *Student 1*—A substitute teacher

Student 2—Him or herself

Student 3—Him or herself

Your teacher is not feeling well and had to stay at home for the day. You and your friend have been asked by the principal to make the substitute feel welcome. Introduce yourselves to the substitute teacher and then explain to them how things work in your classroom.

Tips and Tricks

Younger students such as those between the ages of 5 and 8, may need more guidance when beginning this activity. Guiding them step-by-step will help them remember each part of a proper introduction until they have the procedure memorized. Older students, depending on their life experiences, may find this one easier. To take this exercise a step further, encourage the people who are being introduced to practice their handshaking skills as part of the introduction process. In our culture, handshakes almost always accompany an introduction; so, this is a great time to create an automatic link between handshakes and introductions.

Ideas for Your Own Classroom

_____

_____

_____

8. Practice Special Handshakes

> **Goal:** Show students how to have a little fun while practicing handshakes. This activity will provide students with an opportunity to practice the social skills learned through previous morning meetings in a less formal manner.

Background Knowledge

Videos of teachers greeting their students with special handshakes have dominated social media sites for quite some time and with good reason! They are lots of fun and a great way to socialize with your students. This activity gets your students thinking about creative ways to shake hands and forces them to work on their time management skills, too.

Procedure

- Tell the students that they will be creating a special handshake with their partners today. How they do it is completely up to them, but they will only have five minutes to work on it. Also tell them that they will be showing their special handshake to the class at the end of the meeting.

- Pick sticks to determine which students will work together.

- When you give the start signal, have the students create and practice their special handshake. Don't forget to set a timer!

- Ask all of the students to return to the starting formation and sit next to their partners. Pick as many sticks as you would like. The names of the people you choose will stand up with their partner and present their special handshake to the group.

Tips and Tricks

Challenge your students to add in some facial expressions, chants, or dance moves to their special handshake. This is a great opportunity for your students to add in a little bit of coordination and movement! For students with sensory issues, the above ideas can be used in place of physical touch.

Ideas for Your Own Classroom

_____

_____

_____

_____

_____

_____

_____

_____

_____

_____

_____

_____

_____

_____

9. Greetings Galore

Goal: Encourage students to have a bank of greetings to use when they interact with other people. This bank will prove helpful in many different types of social networking situations where students will have to either introduce themselves or others.

Background Knowledge

Greeting someone politely is a sign of respect and shows people you acknowledge their presence. Greeting someone positively sets the tone for your mutual interaction. Using a wide variety of greetings can be useful when interacting with people of various ages, cultures, and stages of life. Greetings may also vary depending on the time of day.

Procedure

- Ask students to get into the starting formation. Go around the formation and ask each student to provide you with some words or phrases they use to greet people. Using chart paper, a whiteboard, or an interactive board, jot down their responses.

- Add some of your own examples after everyone has had a turn to speak. You can use the following:

  — Hi!

  — Hello! How are you today?

  — Good morning! Good afternoon! Good evening!

  — It is nice to meet you!

  — I am so happy to see you again!

- Pick sticks and place your students into groups of two. After you give the start signal, ask students to begin practicing their greetings.

- When your students have completed the task, ask them to return to the starting formation. For the next part of the exercise, guide your students through greetings in different scenarios. For example, you can pretend that you are a customer at a fast food restaurant and your student is the person taking your order. Or, you can pretend to be a student while your student pretends to be a teacher. The possibilities are endless!

Tips and Tricks

It is important to have older students practice greeting people in positions of authority in various settings. For example, scenarios such as an after-school job interview, a tryout for a sports team, or a volunteer opportunity in the community. In these scenarios, it is helpful to introduce the proper use of titles such as Mr., Ms., Mrs., Dr., Sir, Ma'am, and any other titles that are relevant to their culture.

Ideas for Your Own Classroom

10. I Love Your Smile

Goal: Encourage your students to smile at others and increase their comfort level in doing so in the process. Students will learn that by providing a smile to someone they are meeting for the first time or as a habitual greeting signals to others that the tone of the encounter will be friendly.

Background Knowledge

Smiling at someone is a wonderful way to make someone happy. Although we think it is easy to smile, a lot of people are uncomfortable or self-conscious when smiling at others. Today's activity helps students think about smiling while trying NOT to! Sit back and watch the fun unleash with this one!

Procedure

- On chart paper, a whiteboard, or a Smart Board, write the following two sentences:
    - Speaker 1: "Smile, baby, and tell me that you love me."
    - Speaker 2: "I love you, baby, but I just can't smile."

- Have the students practice saying each sentence aloud.

- This activity works best when played with the whole group. Start the game with the help of one of your students. Pick a stick and place yourself in front of that student while everyone else is in the starting formation.

- Speaker 1 may smile, laugh, stare intently into Speaker 2's eyes, or do something silly during the delivery of their sentence, but speaker 2 must NOT! If Speaker 2 refrains from smiling or laughing, they are declared the winner. If Speaker 2 does not laugh or smile, Speaker 1 continues through the group of students until someone laughs or smiles. If Speaker 2 laughs or smiles, the two players change places and the game continues.

Tips and Tricks

If you do not like the phrases given above, ask your students to say bad dad jokes to each other. The following are examples of bad dad jokes your students could use.

• What do mermaids wash their fins with?
Tide.

• What kind of car does an egg drive?
A Yolkswagon.

• What was the foot's favorite type of chips?
Dor-i-toes.

The premise is the same. There are many videos and websites on the Internet where you can find these hilarious jokes. Chances are your students know a lot of them already!

Ideas for Your Own Classroom

_____

_____

_____

_____

_____

_____

_____

_____

_____

_____

11. Bringing It All Together

Goal: Review and practice the components of the first 10 morning meetings. This will give your students another chance to practice the skills that they learned and provide them with an opportunity to commit the skills to memory.

Background Knowledge

Educators know that teaching new skills requires a lot of practice and that for something to become an automatic habit, a person must do that activity for at least 66 times. The ideas presented in the first 10 morning meetings are things that students can "practice" both inside and outside your classroom. Today's morning meeting consolidates all of the previously introduced social activities into one bundle to give your students confidence in themselves regardless of the social situation.

Procedure

- Review the social skills taught throughout the past 10 morning meetings. Write them on chart paper, the whiteboard, or the Smart Board for use during the activity.

  — Greetings

  — Eye contact

  — Smiling

  — Introductions

  — Handshakes

  — Active listening

- Pick sticks to have students model positive examples of each with you.

- Using your sticks, break the students off into groups of three.

- Give each group a slip of paper that notes a different social situation (see the social situations provided in Morning Meeting Number 7 or come up with your own). The scenarios that the groups will have to act out will allow them to practice using the social skills discussed at the beginning of the meeting.

- Give the start signal. Students will use this time to work on their scenarios.

- Ask all of the students to return to the starting formation. If time permits, have each group perform their scenario. If not, choose the amount of sticks that you have time for. After each group has finished, ask the other students to state the social skills they saw portrayed by their classmates.

Tips and Tricks

As an educational tie-in, ask older students to prepare their own scenarios during a language or writing class to bring to life during the morning meeting. For younger students, you can break down the scenarios and have them concentrate on one or two specific social skills instead of the entire list. Keep this activity handy! It can be used throughout the year and can be adapted for many different social situations that might arise.

Ideas for Your Own Classroom

_____

_____

_____

_____

_____

12. What Is Bullying?

Goal: Educate students about the signs of bullying and provide them with tools to combat it. Students will be able to identify the signs of bullying and will be provided with a variety of options they can use in order to report any signs of bullying they may witness while at school.

Background Knowledge

Thanks to educators and social programs that are put in place in classrooms around the world, today's students have a greater awareness of what constitutes bullying. Even so, we must provide our students with opportunities to talk about bullying, how it affects them, and how it affects others. They must also practice using strategies to help combat the problem in school and in their communities.

Procedure

- You will need chart paper, a whiteboard, or a Smart Board to write down your students' ideas. Going around the starting formation, ask each student to provide you with an example of bullying. Students, especially younger ones, have a tendency to name people who have hurt them in the past so instruct them to not include names. Once everyone has given an example, use the different colored markers listed below to circle the different types of bullying. Give the description of each type as you circle them. If all six types are not given as examples, you can include them after you have circled all the examples provided by your students.

  — Circle examples of *physical bullying* in red (hitting, punching, kicking, etc.)

  — Circle examples of *verbal bullying* in blue (name calling, teasing, verbal threats, etc.)

- Circle examples of *cyber bullying* in orange (threatening emails, aggressive texts, personal memes intended to insult someone specific, etc.)

- Circle examples of *relational bullying* in yellow (exclusion, gossiping, spreading rumors, etc.)

- Circle examples of *sexual bullying* in green (making comments about physical or developmental growth, sexual preference, gender norms, etc.)

- Circle examples of *prejudicial bullying* in brown (making negative or derogatory comments about someone's religion, skin color, race, etc.)

- Going around your starting formation again, ask students what they can do if they are experiencing any type of bullying and what they can do to get help. Here are some examples that you can add if your students do not name them:

  - Tell a parent, teacher, or someone you trust.

  - Show any notes, emails, text messages, and so on, to an adult. Do not destroy or delete them.

  - Practice saying "No" and "Stop" with authority and conviction.

  - Keep an account of where and when the violence is happening. Also keep track of who is doing the bullying.

  - Protect your online presence. Keep passwords protected and social media profiles private.

Tips and Tricks

Students in kindergarten through grade 2 do not need to know all six types of bullying. Concentrate on the ones they will easily understand and identify. For older students, use this morning meeting to offer a time and place where students can come and talk to you in private if they are being bullied or know of someone who is.

Ideas for Your Own Classroom

13. How Does Bullying Affect You?

> **Goal:** Encourage students to share their experiences of being bullied and discuss how bullying affects their well-being. Providing students who are experiencing bullying—or who have been bullied in the past—with a platform to openly and safely talk about the effects bullying has on them, empowers students to take a stand against what is, or has, happened to them.

Background Knowledge

All students have been affected by bullying in some way or another. Educators encourage students to tell an adult whenever they are bullied. Today's morning meeting provides your students with an opportunity to voice their experiences about bullying in a safe environment. They can also use this time to let others know how bullying has affected them.

Procedure

- Have your students get into the starting formation. Review the steps for actively listening as the students will be sharing personal information.

- Share with your students a personal account of having been bullied or where you saw bullying occur. Without naming specific people, add as much detail as you can, including how you felt during and after the incident. It is important for your students to experience the emotions associated with the events and to see how it has affected you. Since today's morning meeting is on a more personal level, I suggest asking for volunteers instead of picking sticks. You will see that the sharing of your story will encourage students to open up and share their own.

Tips and Tricks

When students talk about issues that deeply affect them, some share their experiences freely while others do not. The rules for active listening and for morning meetings in general are incredibly important when hosting meetings like these. Although all students may not feel comfortable sharing their personal experiences, if we provide our students with opportunities to listen attentively while others are speaking, all students will come away from this meeting knowing that they are not alone and that others really do understand how they are feeling.

Ideas for Your Own Classroom

_____

_____

_____

_____

_____

_____

_____

_____

_____

_____

_____

_____

_____

14. Demonstrate What Anger Looks and Feels Like

Goal: Teach students that anger is a common emotion that we all feel from time to time and lead a healthy discussion about what anger looks and feels like. Many students are reprimanded for showing anger in school settings because they do not have the proper skills to deal with their anger properly. This morning meeting will help destigmatize a student's natural reaction to anger and provide them with tools to deal with that emotion in a school setting.

Background Knowledge

Everyone experiences anger. Our students need to know that feeling angry is a normal part of our emotional selves. Today's morning meeting gives students an opportunity to discuss how they feel and behave when they are angry and what triggers that emotion.

Procedure

- Ask students to get into the starting formation. Pick sticks to ask students to give you examples of what happens to our bodies when we are angry. Here are a few examples to help the discussion along:

  — Face turns red

  — Body temperature rises

  — Ears ring

  — Start to cry

  — Clench teeth or fists

  — Stamp your feet

  — Yell

- Break your students into groups of four. When you give the starting signal, challenge the students to share with each other what happens to their bodies when they become angry.

- When you observe that the students have finished sharing, ask everyone to come back to the starting formation. Pick sticks for people to share the physical and emotional feelings their group discussed when they are angry.

Tips and Tricks

For students who are having difficulty talking about how their body reacts to anger, ask them to act out their reactions. For students in middle school and high school, you can expand this activity by asking them to reflect upon how their anger affects those around them.

Ideas for Your Own Classroom

_____

_____

_____

_____

_____

_____

_____

_____

_____

_____

15. Use Calming Techniques

Goal: Teach students calming techniques that they can use when they feel stressed, upset, frustrated, or angry. These techniques, when practiced and implemented, will help students control their behavior in structured situations such as the classroom, and unstructured environments such as the playground and lunchroom.

Background Knowledge

Students have the capability of showing and expressing their anger in many different ways. What many of our students lack is the techniques to self-regulate and calm themselves down. This morning meeting introduces students to some calming strategies to use when feeling overwhelmed.

Procedure

- Ask your students to get into the starting formation. Tell the students that they will continue discussing the previous morning meeting about anger.

- Pick sticks and have those students give you some examples of calming strategies they know of or use themselves.

- Using the examples of your students, of your own, or of the ones included below, model for your students each calming strategy.

  — Count to 10

  — Take a deep breath

  — Tense up every muscle in your body for 30 seconds

  — Ask for a break

  — Stretch your arms and legs

  — Meditate

- While in the starting formation, ask your students to practice each technique for the remainder of the meeting.

Ideas for Your Own Classroom

16. Acknowledge Personal Strengths

Goal: Have each student acknowledge their personal strengths and hear their teacher talk about everyone in the class in a positive light. All students will feel a sense of personal self-worth when hearing positive things said about them by their teacher and classmates. This morning meeting forces everyone to think of positive things to say about each other; even those students who might not usually talk or socialize with one another.

Background Knowledge

Many of our students struggle with positive self-image. Today's morning meeting gives each student an opportunity to hear something positive about themselves from one of the biggest influences in their lives… YOU!

Procedure

- Direct your students to get into the starting formation.

- Pick sticks and talk about each student randomly, or go through the formation one by one. Regardless of the method you choose, make sure to include every student in this exercise and do not mistakenly leave a student out.

- Take your time and speak directly to each student in your class. Look directly into each child's eyes, say their name, and say something positive about them. Below are some sentence starters that can help you.

— *Student,* I am very proud of the way you…

— *Student,* I love the way you…

— *Student,* you always find a way to make me smile!

— *Student,* you are the best at…

— *Student,* I am impressed with the way you…

Tips and Tricks

Your students may feel uncomfortable during this exercise, and that discomfort may be shown with giggling, fidgeting, and in some cases, tears. Please remember that for some of your students, these may be the first kind words they have heard in a long time. Embrace these moments! Allow your students to revel in their emotions, and use this time to form a positive connection with each child.

Ideas for Your Own Classroom

_____

_____

_____

_____

_____

_____

_____

_____

_____

_____

_____

_____

_____

_____

_____

_____

_____

17. Lift Up Others

Goal: Encourage students to look for the good in other people and share those sentiments with others. By focusing on the positives of each person, the perceived mindshift that each of us have of one another will drastically change, thus beginning of change in attitude the teacher and students have of one another.

Background Knowledge

Today's morning meeting is a continuation of yesterday's meeting with one exception—the students will be the ones to provide each other with positivity. In the last morning meeting, you provided wonderful examples of how to praise the students. Now it is time for your students to follow your example.

Procedure

- Ask your students to get into the starting formation.

- Pick sticks and group your students into pairs. The students will not be talking to one another until the end of the morning meeting.

- Give the students time to think of something positive to say about their partner. They can use the prompts from the previous morning meeting to guide them.

  — *Student,* I am very proud of the way you...

  — *Student,* I love the way you...

  — *Student,* you always find a way to make me smile!

  — *Student,* you are the best at...

  — *Student,* I am impressed with the way you...

- Pick sticks to determine when each student will have their turn to talk about their classmate. Remind the students to look directly at the person they are talking about, and to speak loudly and clearly for all to hear.

- Congratulate everyone at the end of the meeting for doing such a wonderful job of making everyone feel good about themselves!

Tips and Tricks

To continue sharing the positivity, you can incorporate this into a writing or art activity. Encourage your students to use these new skills with other students, staff members, and family members. By repeating the action, students will gain confidence in their ability to give joy to others wherever they go!

Ideas for Your Own Classroom

_____

_____

_____

_____

_____

_____

_____

_____

_____

_____

_____

_____

18. Use of Technology in the Home

> **Goal:** Learn about your students' personal use of technology at home.

Background Knowledge

Our students have unprecedented access to technology. From cell phones to tablets to televisions to gaming devices, our students are spending more and more time on their devices and less time having meaningful interactions with others. We don't always know what goes on in the homes of our students, but with this morning meeting, you will gain valuable information about the use of devices in your students' homes.

Procedure

- Direct your students to get into the starting formation.

- Ask the following questions to assess the amount of access students have to technology in their home. You might have some questions of your own that you would like to ask.

  - Raise your hand if you have a television in your room.

  - Raise your hand if you have a gaming system in your room... at home.

  - Raise your hand if you have access to the Internet at home.

  - Raise your hand if you have a computer, laptop, or tablet in your room.

  - Raise your hand if you have a cell phone.

  - Raise your hand if you use a device or watch television in your room when you are supposed to be sleeping.

  - Raise your hand if there are rules or limits that you have to respect when using the Internet or a device at home.

- After each question, pick sticks to ask students to provide more information about the questions asked.

Ideas for Your Own Classroom

_____

_____

_____

_____

_____

_____

_____

_____

_____

_____

_____

19. Early Bird or Night Owl?

Goal: Help your students discover and discuss whether they feel more productive early in the morning or late at night. This morning meeting will be more of a benefit to you, the teacher, than to the students themselves. The information you gather during this meeting will help you determine when students might perform better. This information can then be used to help schedule exam times, teacher-directed lesson times, and student-led lessons times.

Background Knowledge

Our students are all on different daily timetables and schedules. Other than the schedule that they follow at school, our students wake up, eat, do extracurricular activities, and go to bed at various times. With these unique timetables, it is difficult for teachers to juggle the various energy levels of the students throughout the day. This morning meeting helps you identify when your students feel most productive so you can use that information when planning your daily lessons and activities.

Procedure

- Introduce your students to the concepts of early birds and night owls.

  - Early birds are people who like to wake up early, are energetic first thing in the morning, and do their best work in the morning.

  - Night owls are people who like to stay up late, are energetic in the evenings, and do their best work at night.

- Tell your students whether you are an early bird or a night owl and explain your reasons why. The more detail you provide, the more details your students will include when they talk about themselves during the meeting.

- Pick sticks and ask each student if they are an early bird or a night owl. Ask them to give you examples of why they consider themselves an early bird or night owl.

Ideas for Your Own Classroom

_____

_____

_____

_____

_____

_____

_____

_____

_____

_____

_____

_____

_____

_____

20. Sleepyheads

Goal: Help students recognize the importance of sleep in relation to academic performance and overall mental health. Knowing approximately how much sleep your students get each night also helps you understand certain behaviors displayed by students such as lethargy, irritability, and lack of focus.

Background Knowledge

Our students lead very busy and complicated lives. Some students travel long distances to get to school each day, some are high performance athletes, and some have part-time jobs outside of school. Some students are dealing with illnesses, family dysfunction, or other difficulties which take precedence over their lives. All of these factors play a huge role in one's sleeping habits. This morning meeting helps educate your students about the importance of getting a good night's sleep and how that benefits them while at school each day.

Procedure

- Ask your students to get into the starting formation. Go around the formation and ask students what time they went to bed last night. Then, ask the students what time they have to get up in the morning to get ready for school.

- Using that information, determine approximately how many hours your students sleep per night. Mention that younger students and teenagers need between seven to nine hours of sleep each night in order for their brains to be fully receptive to learning properly during the day.

- Using sticks, split the students up into groups of four. Give each group a piece of paper and have them fold the paper in half. On one side of the fold, have them label the side *Not Enough Sleep* and on the other side *Enough Sleep*. When you give the start signal, have your students brainstorm how they feel, or how their bodies react, when they get enough sleep versus when they don't.

- When the students have finished brainstorming, have them return to the starting formation. Pick sticks to have the students share their ideas. Look for common ideas that occur between groups.

Tips and Tricks

Have your students talk about the sleep patterns of their family members, too. This can be an excellent lead-in to a discussion about how different employment or life circumstances can lead to a variety of sleeping arrangements. For older students, this can also be a topic of discussion when thinking about possible career paths.

Ideas for Your Own Classroom

_____

_____

_____

_____

_____

_____

_____

_____

21. Keep Those Energy Levels Up

Goal: Provide students with a variety of strategies to help them get through the midday slump. These strategies will help students regain their focus when they experience a low in their energy levels and will help provide oxygen to their brains.

Background Knowledge

Studies have shown that people tend to feel sleepy, or sluggish, after eating lunch and our students are no exception. Today's morning meeting provides students with a bundle of strategies to use in order to kick-start their energy levels and get them through the rest of the school day.

Procedure

- Ask your students to get into the starting formation. Pick sticks and ask students at what time of the school day they feel sluggish. Ask them to tell you how their bodies feel when their fatigue sets in. The following are examples you might want to contribute to the discussion:
  - Eyes feel heavy
  - Shoulders slump
  - Yawning
  - Difficulty concentrating
  - Body feels heavy

- Break your students into groups of four. When you give your starting signal, have your students brainstorm ways that they can beat the fatigue they feel during class.

— When the students have finished brainstorming, have them return to the starting formation. Pick sticks to have the students share their ideas. Look for commonalities that occur between the groups. The following are examples you might want to contribute to the discussion:

— Ask for a brain break

— Drink water

— Stretch your arms, legs, and upper torso

— Sit up straight

— Eat foods for breakfast and lunch that are high in energy such as bananas and other fresh fruits

Tips and Tricks

It is important to recognize when your students are experiencing a "low" in their energy levels. These lows do not only happen after lunch time. They can happen after an evaluation, a physical education class, or after a hot and humid recess. Encourage your students to bring a water bottle to class and drink from it at regular intervals. Keeping your students hydrated is one of the quickest, easiest, and healthiest ways to keep their energy levels up!

Ideas for Your Own Classroom

_____

_____

_____

_____

_____

_____

22. Kick-Start the Day with a Dance

Goal: Use movement to kick-start the day.

Background Knowledge

It is hard to find someone who doesn't love music! Today's morning meeting features songs with kid-friendly lyrics to get your students to use their listening skills and move around and have fun!

Procedure

- Ask your students to get into the starting formation. Introduce the song that they will be dancing to and the special movement they will be doing whenever they hear the "secret" word or phrase in the song. Your starting signal for this morning meeting will be the song itself.

  - **Around the World**—Daft Punk. Every time "around the world" is said, students move one step to the left while in a circle formation. During each break in the lyrics, students dance on the spot and then change movement directions to the right. Continue until the end of the song.

  - **Come and Get Your Love**—Redbone. Students hold hands in a circle formation. Have them dance in their places until they hear "come and get your love." At that prompt, everyone dances into the middle of the circle while raising their hands up to the ceiling. When they hear it again, instruct them to move back to the circle. Continue until the end of the song.

  - **Get Low**—Dillon Francis and DJ Snake. Students progressively move closer to the floor each time they hear the lyrics "get low." When the music picks up, they can return to a standing position. Continue until the end of the song.

  - **Cupid Shuffle**—Cupid. Follow the directions in the song.

- Ask your students if they know any songs that have repetitive lyrics or ones that are accompanied with a dance. You will be amazed at the songs your students suggest!

Tips and Tricks

This activity is very versatile. Feel free to use any song and movement in your classroom. If you want your students to express their creativity, you can have them make up their own movements. For students in kindergarten to grade 2, younger students, you might want to use activities that focus on gross motor skills and coordination. This morning meeting also serves as a brain break when your students are getting a little sluggish!

Ideas for Your Own Classroom

_____

_____

_____

_____

_____

_____

_____

_____

_____

_____

23. Thinking on Your Feet

Goal: Get students to use their vocabulary skills to make word associations and learn to think quickly on their feet. This activity is a great way to have students make word associations, use their working memory skills, and practice their active listening skills.

Background Knowledge

This game is fast-paced and challenging—even for adults! Timing is everything and those who listen carefully, think quickly on their feet, and have a good vocabulary will be victorious!

Procedure

- Ask all students to stand in a circle for this activity.

- The object of the game is to be the last one standing. Start the game by saying a word. The student to your right will have three seconds to come up with one word that is associated in some way with the word you said. This continues around the circle until someone either repeats a word or says a word that does not have any association with the previous word. Be prepared to make judgment calls. Students who cannot make an association within three seconds, or repeat a word, or choose a word that has no association to the previous word, should sit down. The last student standing is the winner.

- An example of this game is as follows:

  — music—pop—soda—liquid—water—shower—rain, and so on.

Tips and Tricks

This game is perfect for English language learners. In this type of classroom, the teachers would start the game for the students by announcing a topic. For example, the teacher declares *colors* as the topic. All students would then name colors. Other examples of potential topics include the letters of the alphabet, nouns, countries, count by twos, fives, and so on. This game can be used for any subject as a warm-up activity or as a brain break.

Ideas for Your Own Classroom

_____

_____

_____

_____

_____

_____

_____

_____

_____

_____

_____

_____

24. Two Truths and a Lie

Goal: Help students recognize how our body language changes when we are being dishonest. This activity will teach children to acknowledge how their own body feels when they are being dishonest, but to also recognize the signs when someone is being dishonest with them.

Background Knowledge

Whether we like to admit or not, everyone lies. This activity gets students talking about themselves and aware of how their bodies react when they are not telling the truth.

Procedure

- Instruct your students to get into the starting formation. Model this activity for your students. Tell them that you are going to say three things about yourself or something you have done, and that one of the statements is false. Encourage the students to concentrate on your body and facial expressions while you are talking.

- Pick sticks and ask students which statement they think is a lie. If a student guesses incorrectly, continue with the sticks until a student guesses correctly.

- Ask the student what made him or her think that you were lying. Common body language associated with lying includes:

  — Face turning red

  — Inability to look someone in the eyes

  — Fidgeting with one's hands or feet

  — Smiling

  — Nervous laughter

- Have each student think of two things about themselves that are true, and one thing that is false. They must not share this information with anyone just yet.

- Using your sticks, ask one student to give their statements. Tell the other students to observe their body language to see if they can figure out which statement is a lie.

Tips and Tricks

To avoid having students shout out the moment they feel someone is lying, pick sticks to choose one student to give you the answer. If that student is correct, ask the student how he or she knew the person was lying. If the student does not guess properly, choose another stick to give someone else a chance to answer.

Ideas for Your Own Classroom

_____

_____

_____

_____

_____

_____

_____

_____

_____

_____

_____

_____

_____

25. The Importance of Being Honest

Goal: Help students recognize what honesty means and how important it is, when interacting with friends and family. This activity will teach children to acknowledge how their own body feels when they are being honest, but to also recognize the signs when someone is being honest with them.

Background Knowledge

The previous morning meeting introduced students to the signs people give when they are lying. Today's morning meeting focuses on the importance of being honest and truthful.

Procedure

- Ask your students to get into the starting formation. Review yesterday's activity that focused on observing people's body language to determine if they are being truthful or not.

- Explain that yesterday's morning meeting was a game where they had to be dishonest on purpose. Today's morning meeting, on the other hand, focuses on what it means to be honest and how it is defined.

- Pick sticks and ask students what it means to be honest. Record their answers on chart paper, a whiteboard, or a Smart Board. Some answers you can expect to hear are:

  — Telling the truth

  — Following the rules and/or the law

  — Being open about what you are doing or have done

  — Admitting your actions

  — Explaining how a situation truly happened

- Provide your students with a variety of situations, or use the examples below. By picking sticks, ask students how they should respond if they are being honest in each situation.

  — You are playing with a ball inside of the house. You throw it and break a mirror. How could you be honest in this situation?

  — Your friend has a toy that you really like. He left it on his desk at the end of the school day and you decide to put it in your school bag and put it back tomorrow morning before anyone notices. How could you be honest in this situation?

  — You hear some of your classmates speaking badly about another student at school. How could you be honest in this situation?

  — You want to play video games but your parents have asked you to do your homework. You tell them that you have already finished it, even though you still have one chapter to read. How could you be honest in this situation?

- Use your students' answers to spark conversations about the various scenarios.

Tips and Tricks

Your students will react to these situations in a variety of ways, depending on their values and beliefs. It is important not to shame the students for the answers they provide— after all, they are being honest with you.

Ideas for Your Own Classroom

_____

_____

_____

_____

_____

26. When Is a Lie Not a Lie?

Goal: Differentiate between a lie used to surprise someone and one intended to deceive someone. Students will learn that not all non-truths are said with bad intentions.

Background Knowledge

Students need to be able to tell the difference between harmful lies and ones that are said for the benefit of others. This may seem like a weird concept, but there are times when people hide information or mislead others without bad intent. Today's morning meeting challenges students to differentiate between the two.

Procedure

- Instruct your students to get into the starting formation. Pick sticks and ask your students if they think there is ever a good reason to tell a lie.

- Using chart paper, a whiteboard, or a Smart Board, write down the following characteristics of being dishonest:

  - Deceiving someone without taking their feelings into account
  - Withholding information to exclude someone from something
  - Cheating
  - Stealing

- Provide your students with a variety of situations, or use the examples below. By picking sticks, ask the students if they feel these situations are lies or not. Redirect your students to the checklist above to help them decide.

  - You and best friend want to go to see a movie that is rated R. You know your parents will not allow you to go to that movie so you tell them that you are going to a different one.
  - You are planning a surprise birthday party for your brother. When he asks you if you are planning a party for him you reply no.

— Your friend did not study for her exam. She asks you for an answer during the exam and you give it to her.

— You ask your father for money to buy a new game and he says no. While he is in the shower, you go into his wallet and remove his money without his permission.

— Your friend just bought a new outfit and she asks you your opinion about it. You really do not like it but you tell her that it looks great on her.

— You have not seen your grandparents in a long time. On the phone, they tell you that they can't wait to see you next month. However, they show up to surprise you the next day.

• Use your students' answers to spark conversations about the various scenarios.

Tips and Tricks

This activity is meant to show students that in some situations, people withhold the truth in order to surprise someone and make them happy. Honesty is always the best policy, even when we might hurt someone else's feelings.

Ideas for Your Own Classroom

_____

_____

_____

_____

_____

_____

_____

27. Who Can I Trust?

Goal: Help students identify the people in their lives they trust and who to go to when they are in need of help. Students who know who they are able to trust are more likely to seek help when they are in need.

Background Knowledge

Having people you can depend on when you are faced with a difficult situation is critical to our health, safety, and mental well-being. Today's morning meeting encourages students to name the people they can trust and identify the reasons why those people are trustworthy.

Procedure

- Have your students get into the starting formation.
- Using chart paper, a whiteboard, or a Smart Board, write down the following characteristics of someone who is trustworthy:
  - They are honest with friends and family
  - They do what they say they will do
  - They have courage to do the right thing
  - They are loyal to their friends and family
  - They keep promises they make
- Pick sticks and have your students name two people they feel are trustworthy. Have the students refer to the list above to provide reasons why they trust the people they chose.
- Have students reflect on how they can show they are trustworthy every day. Pick sticks and have students respond.

Tips and Tricks

For a visual of this concept, take a piece of paper and tear it a little bit. No matter how you try to put it back together, even with tape, the paper will always have a part that is a little different. Losing someone's trust is like that torn paper. It can take a very long time to earn it back once it is lost. Using a visual like this helps students understand the emotional impact of betraying someone's trust.

Ideas for Your Own Classroom

_____

_____

_____

_____

_____

_____

_____

_____

_____

_____

_____

_____

_____

_____

_____

28. Blind Trust

Goal: Demonstrate to students how to put their trust in their classmates in order to complete a task. At some point in their educational journey, students will have to work with others in order to complete a project or assignment. Students who are grouped together must learn how to trust each other in order to successfully complete the assignment well, and to complete it on time.

Background Knowledge

Trust is an important part of interpersonal relationships. Having trust in people helps us feel safe and secure with those around us. Being trustworthy is also a trait that shows others that we care about them.

Procedure

- Pick sticks and break the students into groups of two.

- Pick a student to help you model the activity. Have your student stand a little distance away from you with their back toward you. When you say go, instruct the student to fall backward into your arms. The students will practice catching each other as they take turns falling backward. This is the ultimate exercise in trusting others and showing that you too can be trusted.

- Give your students the starting signal and then have each student take turns falling into the arms of their partner. The distance between the two students does not have to be very wide as long as they are comfortable with both catching and falling.

- When your students have had an opportunity to catch and fall, have everyone return to the starting formation. Pick sticks to have pairs demonstrate their trust falls in one another.

Tips and Tricks

Since this is a physical and potentially dangerous activity, make sure to properly explain and demonstrate the activity. Any student putting a classmate at risk should be taken out of the activity immediately. If some children are afraid to attempt this activity, you can change it up entirely. As an alternative exercise, blindfold students and then ask their partners to carefully lead them around the classroom.

Ideas for Your Own Classroom

_____

_____

_____

_____

_____

_____

_____

_____

_____

_____

_____

_____

_____

_____

_____

29. R.E.S.P.E.C.T.

Goal: Introduce students to the elements of respect so they can show it to others. Being respectful is a social and emotional expectation in society and in the workplace. This morning meeting introduces the elements of respect to students so they can be mindful of how respectful their behavior is when inside and outside the classroom.

Background Knowledge

Being respectful is more than just being nice to someone. Today's morning meeting teaches students about the characteristics of respect and being respectful of others.

Procedure

- Ask your students to get into the starting formation.
- Using chart paper, a whiteboard, or a Smart Board, write down the following characteristics of respect. Pick sticks to ask for examples of each as you go through the list.
  - Using good manners
  - Using appropriate language
  - Being considerate of others' feelings
  - Avoiding the use of physical or verbal violence
  - Dealing with anger in a peaceful way
- Let the students know that they also need to respect themselves. Discuss what that means. Some examples include eating healthy foods, taking care of our personal hygiene, and exercising. Your students may have additional ideas.
- Lastly, let the students know that they also need to show respect for their environment and the environment of others. This includes their home, classroom, school, the outdoors, and so on.

This morning meeting can be expanded to include a nature walk or used in a science class to discuss environmental issues.

Ideas for Your Own Classroom

_____

_____

_____

_____

_____

_____

_____

_____

_____

_____

_____

_____

_____

_____

_____

_____

_____

30. What to Do When I Don't Get What I Want

Goal: Challenge students to explore their actions and words when they do not get what they want. Students will learn how to respectfully control their emotions when they are disappointed with a decision made that is not to their liking.

Background Knowledge

There are many situations where our students do not get what they want. When children are unable to regulate their emotions in these situations, it can cause a lot of tension and negativity in a classroom setting. This activity calls attention to those emotions through a fun, role-playing activity.

Procedure

- Present your students with the following scenario and have them think about their reactions for a moment:

  - You are at a toy store and you see something that you really want. You ask your parents if you can have it and they say no. How do you react?

  - Ask your students to think about how they feel in those moments, what they say, and what they do.

  - Pick sticks and have your students act out how they respond. Have the other students comment about the body language they witness during the reenactment.

  - When the students are finished showing their reaction to their classmates, ask them how they feel. Most students will feel a little silly, not just from acting in front of the class, but knowing that their behavior has brought out that type of reaction in their friends.

Challenge students to see their personal behavior through the eyes of their parents and strangers in various social settings. Using the previous morning meeting, ask the students how they can change their behavior in order to be more respectful to their parents.

Ideas for Your Own Classroom

_____

_____

_____

_____

_____

_____

_____

_____

_____

_____

_____

_____

_____

_____

_____

31. I Am a Good Friend

Goal: Encourage students to discuss the characteristics that make them a good friend to others. Making friends, keeping friends, and being a good friend does not come easily to all students. This morning meeting will provide students who experience difficulty with making and keeping friends a starting point to embrace these new skills.

Background Knowledge

Our students need to recognize the qualities that make them good friends and positive influences on others. This morning meeting also provides students with an opportunity to hear and say nice things about others in the class.

Procedure

- Ask the students to think about the qualities they have that make them a good friend. Pick sticks and have the students provide their answers to the group.

- Pick sticks again and ask the students to give you examples of how they have been a good friend to someone.

- Pick two sticks at a time. Give the students time to think of something positive to say about their partner. The person with Stick A has to say something about the person with Stick B in regard to being a good friend. Students can use the following prompts if they are having trouble getting started:

  — *Student* shows me *they* are a good friend by...

  — *Student* was a good friend to me when...

  — *Student* is my friend because...

Ideas for Your Own Classroom

_____

_____

_____

_____

_____

_____

_____

_____

_____

_____

_____

_____

_____

_____

32. My Responsibilities

Goal: Discover what your students are responsible for at home and reinforce the responsibilities they have in their school and classroom. Students will benefit from learning the responsibilities of others and take pride in sharing with others what they are responsible for in their own homes.

Background Knowledge

The level of responsibilities your students have may surprise you—either positively or negatively. This morning meeting gives you a chance to learn more about your students' home lives and review the responsibilities they have as a member of your classroom and school community.

Procedure

- Ask your students to get into the starting formation.

- Going around the starting formation, ask students about the responsibilities they have at home. Some examples you may hear are:

  — Wash the dishes

  — Make the bed

  — Feed the family pet

  — Take out the garbage

  — Do one's homework

  — Take care of siblings

  — Work hard at an extracurricular activity

- Going around the starting formation again, ask the students about the responsibilities they have at school. This is a great opportunity to review your school and classroom rules.

To further the conversation about responsibilities, lead the discussion toward the consequences your students face when they do not follow through on their responsibilities at home or at school. For older students who may have part-time jobs, you can expand the discussion even further.

Ideas for Your Own Classroom

_____

_____

_____

_____

_____

_____

_____

_____

_____

_____

_____

_____

_____

_____

_____

33. My Strengths

Goal: Motivate your students to talk about their strengths. This provides your students with an opportunity to speak confidently about themselves in a safe and respectful environment. Many will find this activity difficult because speaking highly of ourselves can often be interpreted as bragging. However, as your students become older, they will be placed in situations such as job or college admission interviews, where they will have to talk about their personal strengths with confidence and pride. Your classroom is the perfect gateway to get your students talking about themselves in a positive light.

Background Knowledge

While in class, students often do not have a chance to talk about their personal strengths. Instead they are asked to talk about the positive traits of characters introduced in stories or books. In today's morning meeting, students use the skills they have been taught to discuss characters and, in turn, to speak positively about themselves.

Procedure

- Going around the starting formation, ask students to state some positive personality traits. This is a great time to review some of the topics discussed in previous morning meetings.

- Model for your students by talking about three of your strengths. Make sure to provide a wide variety of examples and anecdotes to get your students thinking about their own strengths.

- Pick sticks and have your students provide three of their personal strengths. You can help them elaborate by asking questions or prompting them to include more details. You will learn a great deal about your students today!

Tips and Tricks

Some students may not want to give you examples of their strengths, but it is very important that they participate in this activity. For those who are experiencing difficulty talking about themselves, you can help them by providing a strength that you see in that student. You can also ask their classmates to provide examples.

Ideas for Your Own Classroom

_____

_____

_____

_____

_____

_____

_____

_____

_____

_____

_____

_____

_____

_____

_____

_____

_____

34. My Weaknesses

Goal: Introduce students to the idea that everyone has weaknesses, or parts of their character that are less appealing than others. It is also important to help students realize that we, as humans, are flawed and that we are not perfect all the time. Students need to be able to self-reflect and acknowledge parts of their personalities that are less desirable. This will, in time, have students reflect upon ways that they can make changes to those less-desirable qualities.

Background Knowledge

We all have weaknesses that need to be acknowledged and improved. This morning meeting encourages students to explore the weaker aspects of their personalities.

Procedure

- Going around the starting formation, ask students to name some of the more negative qualities of individuals. The following are some examples your students might come up with:

  — Impatience

  — Disorganization

  — Tardiness

  — Forgetfulness

- Start the conversation by talking about three of your weaknesses. Make sure to provide a wide variety of examples and anecdotes to get your students thinking about their own weaknesses

- Pick sticks and have your students provide one, two, or three of their personal weaknesses. You can help them elaborate by asking questions and probing for more details.

Tips and Tricks

You may have some students who do not want to give you examples of their weaknesses but it is very important that they participate in this activity. For students who are unwilling to talk about themselves, you can help them by providing them with ideas. Make sure these ideas are general and vague, so that they do not feel like they are being picked on or put on the spot in front of their classmates.

Ideas for Your Own Classroom

_____

_____

_____

_____

_____

_____

_____

_____

_____

_____

_____

_____

_____

_____

35. The Importance of Flexibility

Goal: Help students understand that in order to work with others, they need to adapt and collaborate in order to be successful. This morning meeting will challenge students to take the needs of others into consideration when working collaboratively. This ability is a necessity when social networking with others.

Background Knowledge

This activity is a great lesson in the importance of being flexible while working with others and it will get your students up and moving!

Procedure

- Describe what it means to be flexible when working with others. Some ideas you might want to include are:

  — Learn to cope with change

  — Listen to other opinions

  — Be open to trying new things

  — Make decisions that are best for the group and not just yourself

- Show your students how to be flexible like a tree. Stand up straight with your feet firmly on the ground. Your feet and legs represent the roots and trunk of a tree. Place your arms like they are branches of the tree. Explain to your students that trees must bend and sway in the wind in order to protect themselves from breaking. Model that action for them.

- Give your students the start signal. Have them find a place around the room where they can become "rooted." Like a tree with its trunk and roots firmly in place, have the students practice swaying in the wind. At your signal, have the students sway from side to side and back to front like a tree does in the wind.

- While students are acting as trees, ask them what would happen if they were unable to bend. They would either break or fall over.

Tips and Tricks

To further demonstrate the importance of flexibility in groups, ask your students to form a line, either side by side or one in front of the other. Have the students complete the same activities, but this time, draw their attention to how flexibility touches everyone in the group. This is a great example that shows how sometimes people in groups over compensate for the lack of flexibility in others.

Ideas for Your Own Classroom

_____

_____

_____

_____

_____

_____

_____

_____

36. Emoji Madness

Goal: Teach students to identify emotions with emojis. Providing students with a visual representation of what they are feeling is an effective way to having students identify their emotions and look for positive solutions for dealing with them.

Background Knowledge

Our students are the most technologically advanced generation ever. Most of them have easy access to the Internet whether it be through a computer, tablet, or telephone. The use of these devices is here to stay, so we need to embrace the technological wave that is in front of us. We can also use this technology to help us connect on a personal level with the children in our classroom.

Procedure

- Ask students to think of an emoji and to keep it to themselves. Ask them to think about the emotions associated with that emoji.

- Pick sticks and ask the chosen students to disclose their emoji, explain why they chose it, and reveal the emotion behind the emoji.

- Ask your students to give you a wide variety of positive and negative emojis. Prompt the students with emotions if they are having difficulty coming up with ideas. For example, the heart eye emoji could indicate that a student really loves or enjoys something while the crying emoji could indicate that the student is sad.

Tips and Tricks

To expand this activity, have your students draw their emojis on a chart paper, whiteboard, or Smart Board and ask the other students to guess the emoji they are drawing. This method adds an element of art to your morning meeting.

Ideas for Your Own Classroom

37. Name That Tune

Goal: Provide an opportunity for students to practice their listening skills by identifying the names of songs hummed by their classmates. This activity provides a chance for your students to communicate with each other using unconventional methods. It forces students to use their listening skills and to try to understand each other.

Background Knowledge

Bringing music into the classroom is a great way to motivate students and get them involved. This activity guarantees that your students will be excited to participate and you will learn a little bit about their musical preferences, too.

Procedure

- Ask your students to think of a popular song but keep it to themselves. Inform them that they will be humming the song to the class to see if others can guess the song.

- Model for the students how to do the activity. Hum something familiar like "Happy Birthday" or "The ABC Song" so that they can easily guess the song. I enjoy using "The ABC Song" because it is also the same melody as "Twinkle Twinkle Little Star." Not many students realize that!

- Pick a stick. That student will hum their song. Pick another stick to choose the student who will guess the song. If the guesser is incorrect, choose another stick. After three wrong guesses, the hummer can reveal their song.

Tips and Tricks

To expand this activity, pair up students or break them into larger groups, to brainstorm songs and hum them together. This makes the activity a little bit harder as the students have to coordinate their timing, pitch, and volume. To facilitate the speed of the activity, prepare pieces of paper in advance with song titles on them so students can randomly pick a song instead of coming up with one on their own.

Ideas for Your Own Classroom

_____

_____

_____

_____

_____

_____

_____

_____

_____

_____

_____

_____

_____

_____

38. What Does a Teacher Do?

Goal: Ask your students to think about the responsibilities a teacher has during the school year. As students learn about all the different responsibilities their teacher has and the amount of time it takes to perform all the tasks associated with the job, the more appreciation students have for their teacher. This appreciation translates into a greater respect shown by the students toward their teacher both inside and outside the classroom.

Background Knowledge

Some people think teachers only deliver curriculum content to students, correct their work, and assign grades. The roles and responsibilities of teachers go way beyond that. This morning meeting gives you a chance to see what your students think your job entails while providing them with details and clarification along the way.

Procedure

- Pick sticks and group your students into groups of four. Provide them with a pencil and a piece of paper.

- Give the starting signal and then ask your students to brainstorm about the roles and responsibilities of a teacher. Have them write their responses on the piece of paper.

- After the students have finished brainstorming, ask them to return to the starting formation with their brainstorming sheets. Pick sticks and ask students to share what is on the sheet.

- When all groups have finished, provide your students with some of the tasks and responsibilities that they did not mention. Some examples include:

  — supervising others

  — ordering educational materials

— organizing field trips

— writing reports

— decorating the classroom and the bulletin boards

— making phone calls

Tips and Tricks

To add an element of drama to this morning meeting, ask students to role-play what they think a teacher does. Have them act as a teacher while they explain what they think are the roles and responsibilities of a teacher. Another option is to have the students play charades and ask them to guess the responsibility being portrayed.

Ideas for Your Own Classroom

_____

_____

_____

_____

_____

_____

_____

_____

_____

_____

_____

_____

39. What Does the Principal Do?

Goal: Ask your students to think critically about a principal's responsibilities during the school year. As students learn about all the different responsibilities their principal has and the amount of time it takes to perform all the tasks associated with the job, they will have more appreciation for their principal. This appreciation translates into showing greater respect toward their principal both inside and outside the classroom.

Background Knowledge

Principals have a wide range of responsibilities that come with their positions. Not many people who work outside of the education field truly understand the job of a school administrator. This morning meeting allows the students to give you their perspective and provides you with an opportunity to give them some insight into the challenging job of a school principal.

Procedure

- Pick sticks and group your students into groups of four. Provide them with a pencil and a piece of paper.

- Give the starting signal and then ask your students to brainstorm about the roles and the responsibilities of a principal. Have them write their responses on the piece of paper.

- After the students have finished brainstorming, ask them to return to the starting formation with their brainstorming sheets. Pick sticks and ask students to share what they noted on their sheets.

- When all groups have finished, provide your students with some of the tasks and responsibilities that they did not mention. Some examples include:

- organizing teacher timetables
- meeting with school board officials
- attending a variety of meetings
- giving permission to teachers to purchase items for the classrooms
- organizing supervision schedules

Tips and Tricks

Why not invite your administrator to participate in this morning meeting? In addition to confirming the responsibilities mentioned by your students, the administrator can provide important insights about running their school. This is a great opportunity for your students to ask questions and to continue to develop a positive relationship with the head of the school.

Ideas for Your Own Classroom

_____

_____

_____

_____

_____

_____

_____

_____

40. Describe the Ultimate Vacation

Goal: Help students verbalize and communicate their ideas through the use of the five W's. Students will practice using who, what, when, where, and why in order to provide greater imagery and detail for those who are listening. Once students are comfortable speaking about a subject and using the five W's, they will be able to transfer those new skills to their writing.

Background Knowledge

For this morning meeting, students will have a conversation with their classmates about where they would like to go on vacation. Encourage your students to use both their imagination and their knowledge to talk about the vacation of their choice.

Procedure

- Using chart paper, a whiteboard, or a Smart Board, write the following prompts for your students:

  — Where will you go?

  — Who will you go with?

  — What will you do when you are there?

  — When will you go?

  — Why that place?

- Model for the students by talking about a vacation that you would like to take if you had an unlimited amount of time and an unlimited budget. Follow the prompts to demonstrate how to use them in the conversation. Elaborate on each of the five W's to show students how to add details to their conversations.

- Pick sticks and break students up into pairs. Give the starting signal. Students will then take turns talking about their ultimate vacation. While Student 1 is speaking, Student 2 can use the listening skills learned in previous morning meetings. When you feel that the conversations are over, ask the students to return to the starting formation.

- Pick sticks once again and have the chosen students share their ultimate vacation ideas with the class.

Tips and Tricks

This activity can be tied to a geography or social studies lesson. Students can take their ideas from this morning meeting and use them to research the destination of their choice. Depending on the age and academic ability of the students, they can also develop an itinerary, make a budget for their vacation, or design a pamphlet to persuade others to travel to their ultimate destination.

Ideas for Your Own Classroom

_____

_____

_____

_____

_____

_____

_____

41. Three Strikes and You're Out!

Goal: Educate your class about the concept of randomness. Some students have difficulty waiting for their turn to speak, some have issues with monopolizing the attention of their teacher and peers, and others have difficulty losing games. Teaching children about how randomness plays an important part in our society shows children that they will not always be first, that they will not always be the center of attention, and that they may not always be the winner.

Background Knowledge

My students love today's morning meeting because they are allowed to stand on their chairs! This game helps students deal with the idea of randomness while they regulate their feelings. With this game, students have no control over the outcome.

Procedure

- Students will not get into the starting formation for today's morning meeting. Instead, ask your students to stay at their desks and stand on their chairs.

- You only need your craft sticks for this game. Randomly pick sticks one at a time. Instruct the person whose name is on the stick to jump down from their chair.

- Place the stick back into the pile. Continue choosing sticks. If a student's name is chosen for the second time, ask that student to sit on their chair. The third time the person's stick is chosen, the student must sit on the floor at this point they are considered out of the game.

- Continue this game until only one person is left standing or sitting on their chair.

Tips and Tricks

If all students do not have access to a stable chair, have them start by standing on their feet. From there, students can move to their knees, and then sit on the floor. It is important that you add the pulled craft sticks back in the pile in order to give a sense of true randomness. To keep the students who are out still interested in the game as it continues, ask them to predict who they think will win the game.

Ideas for Your Own Classroom

_____

_____

_____

_____

_____

_____

_____

_____

_____

_____

_____

_____

_____

42. The Importance of Altruism

Goal: Teach students to think about others before thinking about themselves. Having this personality trait and exhibiting altruism with others will help students be more open and accessible to meaningful social relationships both now and in the future.

Background Knowledge

Altruism is the belief in or practice of selfless concern for the well-being of others. For many students, being altruistic does not come easily. For others, it may come automatically. This morning meeting challenges students to think of the needs of others before thinking of themselves.

Procedure

- Explain to the students what altruism means. Pick sticks and have students provide you with an example of someone being altruistic toward them.

- Continue to pick sticks but this time ask the students to provide you with an example of a time they were altruistic to someone else.

- When these conversations are over, ask students to think about how they would respond to this challenge:

  — You are walking home from school and you find a $20 bill lying on the ground. You are really excited because you can now afford the new book you want. When you get home, you notice that your mom is a little worried. She tells you that she does not have enough money to buy milk and bread that the family needs for breakfast. What do you do? How does your decision make you feel?

- Pick sticks and have the chosen students tell you their decision along with their reasons for making that decision. Encourage the students to tell you how they feel about that decision.

Tips and Tricks

Do not be worried if you notice that some students are struggling with this concept. Depending on their ages and life experiences, students may struggle with identifying the emotions and reasonings beyond being nice to someone. Let students know that it is okay to feel conflicted when faced with such dilemmas. It is also okay to feel disappointed or let down when learning to do the right thing.

Ideas for Your Own Classroom

_____

_____

_____

_____

_____

_____

_____

_____

_____

_____

_____

43. How I Will Change the World

Goal: Encourage students to think about the positive contributions they can make to society. Positively contributing to the classroom and to society promotes a sense of pride within the students. This sense of pride translates into the students' desire to continue making positive contributions daily.

Background Knowledge

Students are frequently asked what they want to do when they get older. Questions like these tend to generate answers that focus on careers, leisure activities, or financial preferences. Today's morning meeting challenges students to put those ideas to the side and instead think about the positive contributions they will make within their families and communities.

Procedure

- Review the meaning of altruism. Pick sticks and place students into groups.

- Have your students discuss among themselves how they will make the world a better place. Ask them to provide examples to their group members.

- When you see that the discussions are finished, ask students to return to the starting formation. Pick sticks and have students explain to the class how they will change the world and how they will go about doing it.

Tips and Tricks

If you want students to think, verbalize, and take action to make change, it is extremely important to validate their ideas. No matter how large or small their idea is, the fact that they have an idea and desire to do great things is remarkable. This validation could be the spark that lights the fire within a student to make positive changes for themselves, their families, and society in general!

Ideas for Your Own Classroom

_____

_____

_____

_____

_____

_____

_____

_____

_____

_____

_____

_____

_____

_____

_____

_____

_____

_____

44. Sweet Smells

Goal: Encourage students to think about smells that trigger pleasant emotions and discuss them with their classmates. This morning meeting will encourage students to think of a positive event and share it with their classmates. This is a wonderful time to take note of what your students value so that you can use that information to help strengthen your personal relationship with them.

Background Knowledge

The sense of smell is very powerful. Many wonderful memories can be brought to the forefront of your mind just from a simple odor. Today's morning meeting encourages students to think about a smell that provokes a positive memory and then share that memory with their classmates.

Procedure

- Going around the starting formation, ask all students to provide you with one example of something they think smells good. Some examples you may hear include food items, perfume, the outdoors, and so on. The sharing of this information will spark many ideas for all students.

- Mention a smell you like and discuss the positive memory that is attached to that smell. Provide details when talking about the smell and the related memories.

- Pick sticks and place the students into pairs. Have them discuss their favorite smells and the memories attached to those odors.

- When you feel the students are done sharing, call them back to the starting formation. Pick sticks and have the chosen students share their memories with the group.

Tips and Tricks

To make this morning meeting hands-on, bring fragrant items such as perfume, vanilla extract, cinnamon, and so on, to your class. Using these items as a warm-up activity can evoke plenty of great conversations. In addition, this may help students think of other smells that remind them of a specific time in their lives.

Ideas for Your Own Classroom

45. Would You Rather...?

Goal: Encourage students to use their critical thinking skills to choose between two different scenarios and to discuss their opinions with others. In society, students will face situations where they will have to give their personal opinion about something. Students need to know that in order to make a well-informed opinion or decision, they must be able to look at the situation from many different angles. This morning meeting will serve as a first taste to thinking critically about different social scenarios and provide them with a chance to practice their critical thinking skills.

Background Knowledge

"Would You Rather" questions are great conversation starters! These questions make students think critically about two really great options or two horrible ones. Be prepared to laugh and have a great time during this morning meeting. You never know what your students will say!

Procedure

- Introduce the "Would You Rather" concept to your students. Tell them that you will present them with two options and that they can only pick one of them. Let them know that they will be asked to justify their answers.

- You can make up your own "Would You Rather" questions or use the following:

  — Would you rather work on math all day or language arts?

  — Would you rather be too hot for five hours or too cold?

  — Would you rather be invisible or be able to fly?

  — Would you rather go to school by giraffe or by donkey?

  — Would you rather use a spoon for all your meals or a fork?

  — Would you rather travel back in time or travel into the future?

- Pick sticks and ask your students to give you their answers to the question. Make sure they elaborate and provide the class with their reasoning behind their choice.

Tips and Tricks

A great enrichment activity for this morning meeting is to think of "Would You Rather" questions that tie into your current curriculum topics. For example, ask questions related to the theme of a novel from your language arts class, pose ethical dilemmas related to social emotional learning, or review social studies concepts.

Ideas for Your Own Classroom

_____

_____

_____

_____

_____

_____

_____

_____

_____

_____

_____

_____

46. Fruit Salad

Goal: Get your students to strategize, move around, and have fun in order to get ready for a full day of learning.

Background Knowledge

The rules of this game are similar to those used in musical chairs. Once students get the hang of it, they can play this game anytime and anywhere as long as there are chairs or sit spots for them to use.

Procedure

- Ask all of your students to sit in a circle with either chairs or in sit spots. Like musical chairs, make sure that there is one less chair or sit spot in the circle than the number of students participating.

- Choose a craft stick. Instruct that student to sit inside the circle and then call out the name of a fruit after you give the start signal.

- Ask the student in the middle to close their eyes while you go around the circle and designate each student as an apple, orange, or pear.

- The game is ready to start once the students have been assigned a fruit. Ask the student inside the circle to open their eyes and call out the name of a fruit (either an apple, orange, or pear). If the student calls out orange, all the oranges must get up and look for another seat. At the same time, the student in the middle, will try to steal the seat of one of the oranges.

Tips and Tricks

To make the game more challenging, ask the student in the middle to call out more than one type of fruit at a time. You can also change this game to a math challenge by assigning numbers to sitting students and have the student in the middle provide equations to be solved.

Ideas for Your Own Classroom

_____

_____

_____

_____

_____

_____

_____

_____

_____

_____

_____

_____

_____

_____

_____

_____

_____

_____

_____

_____

_____

47. For the Love of Pets

> **Goal:** Ask your students to discuss what kind of pets they have and how they care for them. For those students who do not have a pet, ask them to mention the type of pet they would like to have. Talking about pets gives teachers a look into the home life of their students. As well, pets have a positive effect on people, and when students talk about their pets, teachers tend to see a caring, loving, and playful side that they might not normally see in a classroom setting.

Background Knowledge

The impact that pets have on our lives is profound. No matter their shape or size, once a pet enters a home, it becomes an instant member of the family. Pets are also a great way to introduce students to the responsibilities associated with taking care of and providing for another life.

Procedure

- Ask students to raise their hands if they have at least one pet at home. Pick sticks and ask students to give some details about their pets such as names, descriptions, and the responsibilities they have when taking care of them.

- For students who do not have a pet, ask them what pet they would like to have if given that opportunity. Pick sticks and ask students to give you details about which pet they would choose, or why they would choose not to have one.

- Pick sticks and put the students into groups of four. Give the groups time to have a conversation about their pets (or lack thereof). Remind the students to use their active listening skills while waiting for their turn to speak.

Tips and Tricks

Keep in mind that some students might not want to or be able to have a pet. Let students know that this is perfectly acceptable. To keep the conversation flowing with students who do not want to have a pet, ask them to provide you with their reasons why.

Ideas for Your Own Classroom

48. The Alphabet Game

Goal: Encourage students to think quickly about a variety of words encompassing a variety of themes.

Background Knowledge

Much like *"Thinking on Your Feet"* (Morning Meeting #23), this game gets your students thinking on their feet, but in alphabetical order.

Procedure

- Ask all of your students to sit in a circle for this activity.

- Choose one craft stick. The chosen student will be the one to start the game. Ask that individual to say a word that begins with the letter A. Then ask the person sitting next to them to say a word that begins with the letter B, and so on.

- Students have three seconds to give a response. If they are unable to come up with a word within the time limit, or if they repeat a word that has already been said, they must move backward out of the circle.

- The last person to still be in the circle is the winner of the game.

Tips and Tricks

This activity can be modified or adapted in many different ways. Teachers can call out "SWITCH" at any point in the game to make the direction of the game change from clockwise to counterclockwise and vice versa. Teachers can also name themes for each round where the students have to think of a word that fits both alphabetically and within the theme. To really challenge your students, have them begin with the letter Z and work their way through A!

Ideas for Your Own Classroom

49. Growth Mindset

Goal: Help students recognize that through hard work, effort, and a positive attitude, it is possible to increase one's intelligence, talents, and academic level. By changing student mindset and focusing on the positive aspects of their education, students will soon accept the fact that their learning is a journey and that they are capable of persevering when they come up against lessons or concepts that they find difficult.

Background Knowledge

Growth mindset is a hot topic in education. The idea of growth mindset is that through positive actions and thoughts, students can successfully complete hard tasks. One of the easiest ways to start your students on the path to developing a growth mindset is by introducing them to the word YET. This morning meeting will do just that!

Procedure

- Tell the students anecdotes about yourself when you were younger and when you were learning something that was very difficult. Make sure to talk about experiences that took place both inside and outside of school so that your students see how having a growth mindset is important in all aspects of life. For example, you might want to discuss learning how to ride a bicycle without training wheels, memorizing multiplication tables, or running a five-kilometer race without stopping. Be sure to mention what you found difficult about each task, the amount of time, effort, and work you had to put in to achieve your goal, and how you felt after you accomplished what you set out to do.

- Introduce the power of the word *yet* to your students. Yet means that we will be able to have success in the near future. Using the word promotes positive thinking and the expectation that mastery of a task is close at hand. For example, if students are learning multiplication for the first time, they might say, "I haven't memorized my multiplication tables." Learning to add the word yet to the end of the sentence makes the statement more positive and attainable!

- Picks sticks and break students up into groups of four. Have students talk to one other about something they cannot do yet. Make sure that the students use the word *yet* when making their initial statement. In addition, ask them to provide examples of what they will have to do in order to reach their goal.

Tips and Tricks

This morning meeting can extend beyond school-oriented tasks. For example, students may want to talk about relationships with others, extracurricular activities, or goals related to physical or mental health. Whatever your students choose to discuss, make sure that they practice the use of the word *yet* and provide constructive ways in which they can attain their goal. If some students are having difficulty coming up with ideas to attain their goals, offer them suggestions to get their thought processes started.

Ideas for Your Own Classroom

_____

_____

_____

_____

50. Random Acts of Kindness

Goal: Teach students to make a conscious effort to be nice to others. Showing kindness to others is a social networking skill that is required both inside and outside of the classroom.

Background Knowledge

Random acts of kindness are little actions people do every day to make others feel good. These acts of kindness can be done for anyone, anywhere, and for free! With all these positives, there is no reason why random acts of kindness cannot be a part of our daily routines!

Procedure

- Explain that random acts of kindness are gestures people do for others without expecting anything in return. Provide some examples so your students understand the idea behind the term. Also let them know that these acts can be done at anytime, anywhere, and without spending any money.

- Pick sticks and ask the chosen students to tell you about a time when someone did something nice for them. Have them elaborate to tell you who did the action, what it was, and how it made them feel.

- Continue to pick sticks and ask students to think of a time that they performed a random act of kindness. Have them tell you who they did it for, what they did, why they did it, and how they felt doing something nice for someone else.

To provide an additional challenge, write the names of staff members on pieces of paper and place them into a hat. Have each student choose a name from the hat. Ask the students to perform a random act of kindness for the staff member they chose at some point during the week. A few examples include carrying books for the staff member, holding a door open for them, complimenting them on a lesson, and so on. The possibilities are endless!

Ideas for Your Own Classroom

_____

_____

_____

_____

_____

_____

_____

_____

_____

_____

_____

_____

_____

Chapter 5

Starting Your First Closing Circle

Believe it or not, most of the work you need to do to prepare for your very first closing circle is already done! You will be using many of the same procedures used during the morning meetings. There are, however, a few differences. Here are a few tips to help you get your closing circles up and running.

1. Choose an object to pass around the circle (talking tool)

For closing circles, you will only use your craft sticks to choose the student who will begin talking. That student will hold an object of your choosing, also known as a "talking tool," such as a stuffed animal, a trinket, etc.). The student holding the object is the only person who has the right to speak. When the student has finished speaking, they will pass it to the person sitting next to them. This procedure continues until everyone has a chance to contribute to the circle.

2. Introduce the closing circle concept to the class

Explain the concept of closing circles to your students. Let them know that closing circles are held every afternoon before leaving for the day. The difference between morning meetings and closing circles is that all students will have an opportunity to speak before the circle is over and closing circles do not involve groups.

3. Get the classroom ready for the end of the day

Since the closing circle is used as a wrap-up activity for the day, it is important that your students are ready to leave before starting. Ensure all of your classroom materials are put away and that the students' backpacks are packed up and ready to go.

4. Call everyone into circle formation

Closing circles work best when done in a circle formation. Decide where you would like students to sit. If space constraints make it difficult for you to get all of your students into a circle, choose a formation that works best for you.

5. Greeting

Just like with your morning meeting, it is important to greet everyone when they enter the circle. During the first meeting, establish the rules and procedures that you expect your students to follow during closing circle time. You can set these rules yourself or make it a class activity. These rules and expectations will become the foundation of your closing circles.

6. Host the closing circle

Feel free to use the 50 closing circles provided in the next section. The closing circles provided are intended to get you up and running with very little preparation time! You do not have to follow the closing circles in order, although some will be continuations from their morning meeting counterparts.

7. Adjournment

As with any gathering of people, bringing it to a complete close is just as important as opening the meeting. The closing circle adjournment is extremely important because it is the last thing students will hear from you before they are dismissed to go home. Keep the message light and positive! The goal is to have your students leave with smiles on their faces!

And there you have it! You are now ready to start your first closing circle. You will find that these last few minutes of the day will be relaxing and both you and your students will leave on a positive note. No more rushing to get out the door! No more bargaining with students to keep working until the last bell rings! In no time at all, your closing circle will become one of the highlights of your day.

It is very important that you take part in these circles. The more that you open up, participate, and share your ideas, the more your students will trust and respect you!

Ideas for Your Own Classroom

51. What Went Well for You Today?

Goal: Encourage your students to focus on the positives of the day. By focusing on the positive aspects that happened during the day, the teacher gets instant feedback on what the students enjoyed about the day, and the students hear from one another what they appreciated about their time at school.

Background Knowledge

Most of our students are depleted after a full day of rigorous learning. This closing circle gives students a chance to reflect upon the things that went well today at school. It also provides an opportunity to leave school on a positive note.

Procedure

- Pick a stick. This stick represents the student who will begin the discussion in the closing circle that day. Pass the object that you have chosen as your "talking tool" to the person whose craft stick was chosen.

- Begin the closing circle activity by asking the following question: What is one thing that went well for you today? Give your students a few seconds to think about their answer.

- Ask the student whose stick was chosen to respond first and when finished, pass the "talking tool" to the person on the left or the right. This procedure continues until everyone has a chance to speak.

Tips and Tricks

As this is the first closing circle, it might take longer than 10 minutes to complete. Keep this in mind when you are planning your regular lessons. It is important to let the students know that they must think of their responses while they are waiting for their turn to speak. We do not want students to miss their buses, so your closing circles must be done quickly and efficiently.

Ideas for Your Own Classroom

_____

_____

_____

_____

_____

_____

_____

_____

_____

_____

_____

_____

_____

52. What Can You Improve for Tomorrow?

> **Goal:** Encourage students to reflect on their day and think of ways in which they can improve themselves for tomorrow. By having students reflect on what they could improve upon for the next day, students will leave for the day with a plan to do better tomorrow.

Background Knowledge

Our students go through a range of emotions and behaviors during the school day. This closing circle gives students a chance to think about their day in a constructive way and provide them with an opportunity to think of something they want to do better tomorrow.

Procedure

- Pick a stick. This student will begin today's circle. Pass the object that you have chosen as your "talking tool" to the person whose craft stick was chosen.

- Begin the closing circle activity by asking the following question: What can you improve upon for tomorrow?

- Give your students a few seconds to think about their answer.

- Ask the student whose stick was chosen to respond first and when finished, pass the "talking tool" to the person on the left or the right. This procedure continues until everyone has a chance to speak.

Tips and Tricks

This closing circle does not have to be about behaviors or emotions. It can also be a task the student wants to improve. For example, if a student does not think they made the best effort in physical education, they can select that as the area of improvement.

Ideas for Your Own Classroom

_____

_____

_____

_____

_____

_____

_____

_____

_____

_____

_____

_____

_____

_____

_____

53. Show Appreciation

Goal: Ask students to verbalize something about their school that they are thankful for so as to learn how to show their appreciation for something. Often, it is difficult for people to express their appreciation, mostly because they are shy and feel vulnerable. This morning meeting provides students with the opportunity to express their personal opinions in a safe and nurturing environment.

Background Knowledge

School means a variety of things to a variety of people. Some students come to school because they have to. Others come to school because they want to. The focus of this closing circle is to give students the opportunity to tell their classmates something that they are thankful for because of school.

Procedure

- Pick one stick. This student will begin today's circle. Pass the object that you have chosen as your "talking tool" to the person whose craft stick was chosen.

- Begin the closing circle activity by asking the following question: What is something at school that you are thankful for?

- Give your students a few seconds to think about their answer.

- Ask the student whose stick was chosen to respond first and when finished, pass the "talking tool" to the person on the left or the right. This procedure continues until everyone has a chance to speak.

Tips and Tricks

If the children have difficulty coming up with ideas, ask them to think about people who work in the school, various school activities or field trips, or academic tasks they have mastered. One suggestion has the potential to start a flood of ideas.

Ideas for Your Own Classroom

54. Listen to the Sounds All Around the Classroom

Goal: Ask students to reflect on the listening skills they learned in their morning meeting and talk about sounds they heard throughout the day that made them smile. This activity ensures that students leave for the day with a good feeling in their hearts. It also provides the students with a mental visual of something about their school day that made them happy.

Background Knowledge

Schools contain a plethora of external stimuli that can be difficult to process. The morning meeting that corresponds to this closing circle taught students how to power down their other senses in order to let their sense of hearing dominate. This circle allows students to talk about some of the sounds they heard throughout the day.

Procedure

- Pick a stick. This student will begin today's circle. Pass the object that you have chosen as your "talking tool" to the person whose craft stick was chosen.

- Begin the closing circle activity by asking the following question: What sound did you hear today that made you smile?

- Give your students a few seconds to think about their answer.

- Ask the student whose stick was chosen to respond first and when finished, pass the "talking tool" to the person on the left or the right. This procedure continues until everyone has a chance to speak.

Tips and Tricks

To challenge the students, provide them with different areas of the school environment to consider. How do sounds inside the school differ from sounds outside in the playground? What sound inside the school makes them feel happy and relaxed? What sound makes them think of school?

Ideas for Your Own Classroom

55. End the Day with a Good Laugh!

Goal: Provide your students with a good laugh before leaving for the day. In order for students to want to come back to school each day, teachers have to ensure that they leave the school each afternoon on a good foot. One of the best ways to do this is to make sure your students are laughing and smiling at the end of the day.

Background Knowledge

There is no better way to bring students and teachers together than with a good laugh! This closing circle promises to get you and your students laughing at the funny things that happened during the day.

Procedure

- Pick one stick. This student will begin today's closing circle. Pass the object that you have chosen as your "talking tool" to the person whose craft stick was chosen.

- Begin the closing circle activity by asking the following question: What is something funny that happened at school today?

- Give your students a few seconds to think about their answer.

- Ask the student whose stick was chosen to respond first and when finished, pass the "talking tool" to the person on the left or the right. This procedure continues until everyone has a chance to speak.

Tips and Tricks

If students cannot come up with something funny that happened during the day, ask them to think of something funny that happened during the week. This closing circle can get loud and a little out of control—but that is a good thing! Just be careful! The giggling can become contagious!

Ideas for Your Own Classroom

_____

_____

_____

_____

_____

_____

_____

_____

_____

_____

_____

_____

56. The Meeting of a Lifetime

Goal: Discover who your students admire and respect. Whether students admire family members or YouTubers, having this information provides teachers with an opportunity to connect with their students. This information can be used during lessons in order to attract student attention, or can be thrown into casual conversation during recess. The more teachers know about their students, the more easily they can forge relationships with them.

Background Knowledge

Our students look up to many different people from various walks of life. This closing circle provides you with insight into the people your students admire.

Procedure

- Pick a stick. This student will begin the circle for the day. Pass the object that you have chosen as your "talking tool" to the person whose craft stick was chosen.

- Begin the closing circle activity by asking the following question: Who would you like to have a conversation with and why?

- Give your students a few seconds to think about their answer.

- Ask the student whose stick was chosen to respond first and when finished, pass the "talking tool" to the person on the left or the right. This procedure continues until everyone has a chance to speak.

Tips and Tricks

Some students may choose to speak to someone who has passed away. If so, this closing circle could become emotional. Make sure to support any student who chooses to speak about someone they love who has passed on or who is no longer present in their lives. This may be the only opportunity they have to voice their sadness.

Ideas for Your Own Classroom

_____

_____

_____

_____

_____

_____

_____

_____

_____

_____

_____

_____

_____

57. Promote Happiness All Around

Goal: Encourage your students to talk about feelings of happiness that occurred throughout the day. Having students leave on a positive note greatly raises the probability that the students will not only want to come back to school the next day, but will come back to school with a positive attitude.

Background Knowledge

Some students find happiness wherever they go. For others, it is a struggle to focus on the positives of the day. Today's closing circle gives students a chance to reflect upon and talk about one thing that made them feel happy during the school day.

Procedure

- Pick one stick. This student will begin the circle for the day. Pass the object that you have chosen as your "talking tool" to the person whose craft stick was chosen.

- Begin the closing circle activity by asking the following question: What is something that made you feel happy today?

- Give your students a few seconds to think about their answer.

- Ask the student whose stick was chosen to respond first and when finished, pass the "talking tool" to the person on the left or the right. This procedure continues until everyone has a chance to speak.

Tips and Tricks

If you have students who are having difficulty participating in this closing circle, speak for them! Let them know what they did today that made you feel happy. These students might not be able to verbalize how they are feeling, but by doing this you are ensuring that they finish the school day feeling loved and appreciated.

Ideas for Your Own Classroom

58. Stomp Out That Anger

Goal: Erase the day's frustrations and go home on a positive note! For some students, one frustration can ruin their entire day. This closing circle will provide students with an opportunity to rid their minds of any negativity that might have built up so that they can return home happy and want to return to school the next day.

Background Knowledge

There are times throughout the day when we get angry, frustrated, or disappointed. These feelings can be caused by both external and internal forces. Today's closing circle allows your students to verbalize their frustrations so they can go home with a more positive attitude.

Procedure

- Pick one stick. This student will begin the circle for the day. Pass the object that you have chosen as your "talking tool" to the person whose craft stick was chosen.

- Begin the closing circle activity by asking the following question: What is something that made you angry today?

- Give your students a few seconds to think about their answer.

- Ask the student whose stick was chosen to respond first and when finished, pass the "talking tool" to the person on the left or the right. This procedure continues until everyone has a chance to speak.

Tips and Tricks

Add some movement to this circle to create a visual and kinesthetic connection. Have students physically stomp their feet when they share what made them angry. Tell the students that by stomping on their anger, they are getting rid of it for good!

Ideas for Your Own Classroom

_____

_____

_____

_____

_____

_____

_____

_____

_____

_____

_____

_____

_____

_____

_____

59. Saying Goodbye

Goal: Discover what your students do when they have to say goodbye to someone they love. This closing circle is important because it shows the vulnerabilities of both the teacher and the students. Since we never really know what is going on in the homes of our students, this circle may provide a sense of support for students who are dealing with some sort of loss or feelings of loneliness at home.

Background Knowledge

People react differently to different goodbye situations. While some goodbyes are done quickly and daily, other goodbyes are harder and done less frequently. This closing circle gives your students an opportunity to discuss how they handle goodbyes with the people they love.

Procedure

- Pick one stick. This student will begin the circle for the day. Pass the object that you have chosen as your "talking tool" to the person whose craft stick was chosen.

- Begin the closing circle activity by asking the following question: When you are saying goodbye to someone you care about, how do you do it and what do you say?

- Give your students a few seconds to think about their answer.

- Ask the student whose stick was chosen to respond first and when finished, pass the "talking tool" to the person on the left or the right. This procedure continues until everyone has a chance to speak.

Tips and Tricks

This closing circle can be quite emotional for students if they choose to talk about people who have passed away or who they do not see very often. This might especially ring true for children of separated or divorced parents. Others will provide you with heartwarming insights into their personal lives with their families. Keep the circle flowing with understanding and empathy for all the students who participate today.

Ideas for Your Own Classroom

60. Smile!

Goal: Discuss what made students smile throughout the day. This closing circle forces students to concentrate on the positive aspects of the day so that they go home happy with the desire to return to school again the next day.

Background Knowledge

Teachers are always searching for ways to make their students smile. This closing circle provides your students with an opportunity to focus on the positives of the day before leaving for home.

Procedure

- Pick one stick. This student will begin the circle for the day. Pass the object that you have chosen as your "talking tool" to the person whose craft stick was chosen.

- Begin the closing circle activity by asking the following question: What is one thing that made you smile today?

- Give your students a few seconds to think about their answer.

- Ask the student whose stick was chosen to respond first and when finished, pass the "talking tool" to the person on the left or the right. This procedure continues until everyone has a chance to speak.

Tips and Tricks

It is not necessary for students to talk specifically about the game that was played during the coordinating morning meeting. Encourage students to talk about anything that made them smile today. If they are having difficulty coming up with ideas, ask them to think about interactions they had with friends, other students, or staff members.

Ideas for Your Own Classroom

61. I Am Unique!

Goal: Give students and opportunity to talk about something that makes them unique. Many students feel the need to "fit in" with the others around them and tend to think that the characteristics that make them unique are negative. This closing circle will celebrate the characteristics that the students themselves think make them unique.

Background Knowledge

We each have something that makes us unique. It might be something physical, athletic, or down right quirky but whatever it is, it makes us special. This closing circle gives students an opportunity to brag about themselves in front of you and their classmates.

Procedure

- Pick one stick. This student will begin the circle for the day. Pass the object that you have chosen as your "talking tool" to the person whose craft stick was chosen.

- Begin the closing circle activity by asking the following question: What is something that makes you unique?

- Give your students a few seconds to think about their answer.

- Ask the student whose stick was chosen to respond first and when finished, pass the "talking tool" to the person on the left or the right. This procedure continues until everyone has a chance to speak.

Tips and Tricks

Depending on the age of your students, it might be a good idea for you to start this closing circle. That will give your students an idea of what to talk about when describing what makes them unique. Talents, quirks, and superstitions are great examples of things that make people unique.

Ideas for Your Own Classroom

_____

_____

_____

_____

_____

_____

_____

_____

_____

_____

_____

_____

_____

_____

_____

62. What Is Bullying?

Goal: Openly discuss acts of bullying students may have witnessed throughout the day and identify how seeing these acts makes them feel. The teacher will get a sense of the types of bullying witnessed and also the frequency. Think of this as an insider's view to the world of bullying at school.

Background Knowledge

Bullying doesn't just happen in classrooms. Most of the time, bullying at school occurs during unstructured teaching times like recess and the lunch hour. It is also more likely to occur in less supervised areas such as washrooms and hallways.

Procedure

- Pick one stick. This student will begin the circle for the day. Pass the object that you have chosen as your "talking tool" to the person whose craft stick was chosen.

- Begin the closing circle activity by asking the following question: Did you witness an act of bullying today? If so, what was it and how did it make you feel?

- Give your students a few seconds to think about their answer.

- Ask the student whose stick was chosen to respond first and when finished, pass the "talking tool" to the person on the left or the right. This procedure continues until everyone has a chance to speak.

Tips and Tricks

It is important to advise the students that you do not want them to name the bully during the closing circle. Inform your students that you will be available to speak to them at the end of the meeting to get more information regarding the bullying they may have witnessed. Encourage students to use the vocabulary discussed in the coordinating morning meeting when talking about the various types of bullying witnessed.

Ideas for Your Own Classroom

63. Putting a Stop to Bullying

Goal: Help students understand that it is their social responsibility to report any acts of bullying or violence. Often, students are afraid to report incidents of bullying for fear of becoming the next target or being harassed for being a tattletale. This closing circle will reinforce the importance of telling someone when they see or hear any bullying incident.

Background Knowledge

Many times, our students do not report bullying to an adult for fear of being the bully's next target. Today's closing circle gives your students a safe place to talk about actions they have taken to protect a target and ultimately put an end to violence at school.

Procedure

- Pick one stick. This student will begin the circle for the day. Pass the object that you have chosen as your "talking tool" to the person whose craft stick was chosen.

- Begin the closing circle activity by asking the following question: When you witnessed an act of bullying, what did you do to stop it?

- Give your students a few seconds to think about their answer.

- Ask the student whose stick was chosen to respond first and when finished, pass the "talking tool" to the person on the left or the right. This procedure continues until everyone has a chance to speak.

Tips and Tricks

In order to encourage our students to speak out against violence and bullying, it is important to validate the actions they have taken to stop the behavior. Make sure to congratulate them when they talk about what they have done to stop bullying. Show students you are proud of them for making the right choices. This will encourage them to continue to do so in the future.

Ideas for Your Own Classroom

_____

_____

_____

_____

_____

_____

_____

_____

_____

_____

_____

_____

_____

_____

_____

64. Recognizing Our Anger

Goal: Encourage students to talk about something that made them feel angry today. This closing meeting encourages students to acknowledge their angry feelings and talk about what made them feel that way. By talking about it in the circle, students are able to get the feeling off their chests and go home with a more positive outlook.

Background Knowledge

Many students have difficulty regulating emotions when at school. The two biggest emotions children have a hard time controlling are anger and frustration. This closing circle gives students an opportunity to talk about something that made them feel angry during the school day.

Procedure

- Pick one stick. This student will begin the circle for the day. Pass the object that you have chosen as your "talking tool" to the person whose craft stick was chosen.

- Begin the closing circle activity by asking the following question: Did anything make you angry today? What situation were you in and how did you deal with it?

- Give your students a few seconds to think about their answer.

- Ask the student whose stick was chosen to respond first and when finished, pass the "talking tool" to the person on the left or the right. This procedure continues until everyone has a chance to speak.

Tips and Tricks

Let your students know that it is okay to feel anger and that it is a natural emotion that we all experience. Congratulate students for showing self-control in angry situations. Give students an opportunity to talk about what makes them angry. This also gives everyone an idea of what triggers angry emotions in each other.

Ideas for Your Own Classroom

65. Putting Our Calming Techniques to Work

Goal: Get students to acknowledge the calming techniques they used during the day. By giving students a chance to talk about the techniques they learned during the morning meeting, the teacher reinforces key concepts students can use to self-regulate their behavior when their feelings become overwhelming.

Background Knowledge

Your students have learned that feeling angry is a normal emotion. Now it is time for them to start thinking about and applying calming techniques learned in the coordinating morning meeting. This closing circle gets your students to reflect upon the techniques that work best for them and how they can apply them during the school day.

Procedure

- Pick one stick. This student will begin the circle for the day. Pass the object that you have chosen as your "talking tool" to the person whose craft stick was chosen.

- Begin the closing circle activity by asking the following question: What calming technique did you use today?

- Give your students a few seconds to think about their answer.

- Ask the student whose stick was chosen to respond first and when finished, pass the "talking tool" to the person on the left or the right. This procedure continues until everyone has a chance to speak.

Make sure to congratulate your students for sharing what they did to calm down. It is not easy for students to admit when they are angry so the fact that they are sharing this information with you and the class is a great step forward in building classroom community.

Ideas for Your Own Classroom

_____

_____

_____

_____

_____

_____

_____

_____

_____

_____

_____

_____

_____

_____

_____

_____

_____

66. The Kindness Circle

Goal: Encourage students to say something nice about each other. This activity allows all students to hear something nice about themselves from other people. This way, all students go home with positive thoughts in their heads and with a desire to return to school the next day.

Background Knowledge

This closing circle provides an opportunity for your students to compliment each other in a safe and secure environment. Some children feel embarrassed when speaking kindly about others, especially if that person is of the opposite sex.

Procedure

- Pick one stick. This student will begin the circle for the day. Pass the object that you have chosen as your "talking tool" to the person whose craft stick was chosen.

- Begin the closing circle activity by giving the following prompt: Say something nice about the person sitting next to you.

- Give your students a few seconds to think about their answer.

- Ask the student whose stick was chosen to respond first and when finished, pass the "talking tool" to the person on the left or the right. This procedure continues until everyone has a chance to speak.

Tips and Tricks

This circle may be difficult for students who have a hard time speaking positively about others. It is designed in such a way to ensure that all students are given the task of speaking nicely about someone, even those they may not like. This is where you will see your students' integrity shine through.

Ideas for Your Own Classroom

_____

_____

_____

_____

_____

_____

_____

_____

_____

_____

_____

_____

67. Do the Right Thing

Goal: Ensure your students receive positive feedback for their good behavior. Students enjoy being told when they have done something positive. This feedback encourages more of the behavior that prompted the praise in the first place. This type of positive assessment lets students know that you appreciate the efforts they made to follow the rules.

Background Knowledge

Our students have an easier time telling us when someone has done something wrong rather than when someone does something right. This closing circle encourages students to reflect upon the good behavior that they witnessed during the day and give a shout out to those who did the right thing.

Procedure

- Pick one stick. This student will begin the circle for the day. Pass the object that you have chosen as your "talking tool" to the person whose craft stick was chosen.

- Begin the closing circle activity by using the following prompt: Congratulate the person sitting next to you for something positive they did today.

- Give your students a few seconds to think about their answer.

- Ask the student whose stick was chosen to respond first and when finished, pass the "talking tool" to the person on the left or the right. This procedure continues until everyone has a chance to speak.

Tips and Tricks

Challenge yourself to be on the lookout for your students' positive behavior. As an added bonus to this closing circle, take the time to speak about each student in your class. This will let your students know that you are not only checking for positive behavior but that you are also proud of the good choices they made throughout the day.

Ideas for Your Own Classroom

_____

_____

_____

_____

_____

_____

_____

_____

_____

_____

_____

_____

_____

_____

68. Is There an App for That?

Goal: Challenge students to use their imaginations to think of an app that will make their lives easier. This closing circle gives students a chance to talk about something that has nothing to do with curriculum demands but has a great deal of creative freedom. It is the perfect closing circle to have with your students at the end of a hectic learning day.

Background Knowledge

Our students are very creative, but they are not given a lot of time to "think on their feet." Today's closing circle challenges students to do both! By harnessing their love of technology and their creativity, you can sit back and watch your students amaze you with their innovative ideas.

Procedure

- Pick one stick. This student will begin the circle for the day. Pass the object that you have chosen as your "talking tool" to the person whose craft stick was chosen.

- Begin the closing circle activity by asking the following question: What is an app you would invent to make your life easier?

- Give your students a few seconds to think about their answer.

- Ask the student whose stick was chosen to respond first and when finished, pass the "talking tool" to the person on the left or the right. This procedure continues until everyone has a chance to speak.

Tips and Tricks

The focus of this closing circle is for the students to concentrate on themselves and their needs. Listen carefully to their responses. Some might give you direct insight into problems they are struggling with at home or at school.

Ideas for Your Own Classroom

69. Rise and Shine

Goal: Learn about your students' morning weekend routines. This provides you with valuable information regarding the home and personal life of your students outside of your classroom. Knowing this information is an asset when connecting and building relationships with your students.

Background Knowledge

Ever wonder what students do when they wake up on Saturday and Sunday morning? This closing circle gives you insight into your students' morning routines on the days they are not in school. From sports practices to spending quality time with their families, you will learn what your students do before lunch on the weekends.

Procedure

- Pick one stick. This student will begin the circle for the day. Pass the object that you have chosen as your "talking tool" to the person whose craft stick was chosen.

- Begin the closing circle activity by giving the following prompt: Tell us about your morning weekend routine.

- Give your students a few seconds to think about their answer.

- Ask the student whose stick was chosen to respond first and when finished, pass the "talking tool" to the person on the left or the right. This procedure continues until everyone has a chance to speak.

Tips and Tricks

To give your students an idea of what you are looking for, start by telling them about your morning routine on the weekend. Students love to hear about the lives of their teachers. By opening up to your students, you let your students know that they can open up to you.

Ideas for Your Own Classroom

_____

_____

_____

_____

_____

_____

_____

_____

_____

_____

_____

_____

_____

_____

_____

70. Go to Bed, Sleepyhead

Goal: Learn about your students' weekend bedtime routines. This information will give you insight into how much or how little sleep your students average per night. Knowing this information is an asset when connecting and building relationships with your students. It may also help to explain student behavior or performance.

Background Knowledge

Ever wonder what your students do on the weekend? This closing circle gives you insight into the bedtime routine of your students during the days when they are not in school. From staying up late to reading books to spending quality time with their families, you will learn what your students do on the weekends.

Procedure

- Pick one stick. This student will begin the circle for the day. Pass the object that you have chosen as your "talking tool" to the person whose craft stick was chosen.

- Begin the closing circle activity by giving the following prompt: Tell us about your weekend bedtime routine.

- Give your students a few seconds to think about their answer.

- Ask the student whose stick was chosen to respond first and when finished, pass the "talking tool" to the person on the left or the right. This procedure continues until everyone has a chance to speak.

To give your students an idea of what you are looking for, start by telling your students about your bedtime routine on the weekend. Students love to hear about the lives of their teachers. By opening up to your students, you let your students know that they can open up to you.

Ideas for Your Own Classroom

71. Feeling Sluggish

Goal: Identify the times of the school day when your students feel sluggish and come up with ideas on how to combat it. These ideas will help students know when they are feeling low on energy and focus so that they may apply techniques learned in morning meetings to beat the fatigue.

Background Knowledge

Just like teachers, students have times throughout the day where they feel like they are running out of energy. This closing circle provides an opportunity for your students to reflect upon a time during the day when they have difficulty concentrating or staying on task. They will also tell their classmates what they do to energize themselves.

Procedure

- Pick one stick. This student will begin the circle for the day. Pass the object that you have chosen as your "talking tool" to the person whose craft stick was chosen.

- Begin the closing circle activity by asking the following questions: Was there a time during the day when you had difficulty concentrating? What did you do to perk yourself up?

- Give your students a few seconds to think about their answer.

- Ask the student whose stick was chosen to respond first and when finished, pass the "talking tool" to the person on the left or the right. This procedure continues until everyone has a chance to speak.

Tips and Tricks

Ask your students to demonstrate what they do to perk themselves up. For example, if a student says that they take a deep breath to reenergize, ask them to show you how this is done. This provides the student with another opportunity to "wake-up," and it serves as a physical prompt for others to do the same!

Ideas for Your Own Classroom

72. Create a Song Playlist

Goal: Get your students to talk about their favorite songs. This information is useful for teachers because they can use the songs discussed by students in different assignments, and they can be used in a way to make an emotional connection with students.

Background Knowledge

This closing circle gives your students an opportunity to talk about the songs that bring them happiness and joy. Be prepared to hear a variety of songs from a variety of artists. You may just find your new favorite song or artist during today's closing circle!

Procedure

- Pick one stick. This student will begin the circle for the day. Pass the object that you have chosen as your "talking tool" to the person whose craft stick was chosen.

- Begin the closing circle activity by asking the following question: What song makes you want to get up and dance?

- Give your students a few seconds to think about their answer.

- Ask the student whose stick was chosen to respond first and when finished, pass the "talking tool" to the person on the left or the right. This procedure continues until everyone has a chance to speak.

Tips and Tricks

Keep track of the songs your students mention. Use their ideas to make a playlist to be used in your classroom in the future. Bringing music into the classroom is a great way to connect with your students in a variety of ways. When used correctly, music can energize students when they are feeling sluggish or calm them down when they are too excited.

Ideas for Your Own Classroom

73. Think Quickly

Goal: Get your students to think on their feet while having fun! This is a great way to end the day and to send your students home on a positive note!

Background Knowledge

The purpose of this closing circle is to have fun! It is also a great time to review curriculum content.

Procedure

- Pick one stick. This student will begin the circle for the day. Pass the object that you have chosen as your "talking tool" to the person whose craft stick was chosen.

- Begin the closing circle activity by giving the following prompt: When I say go, you have 10 seconds to come up with as many words that begin with the letter ___?

- Give your students a few seconds to think about their answer.

- Ask the student whose stick was chosen to respond first and when finished, pass the "talking tool" to the person on the left or the right. This procedure continues until everyone has a chance to speak.

Tips and Tricks

If 10 seconds is too long, change the amount of time provided to each student. You can also change this activity to incorporate any curriculum content. For example, ask students to skip count, do a vocabulary review, or recite the names of states.

Ideas for Your Own Classroom

74. A Glimpse into the Future

Goal: Encourage your students to think about what their lives will be like in 10 years. This activity is a great way to learn about your students and to see the goals your students have set for themselves. You will also gain insight into what your students like and value. The information you learn about your students from this closing circle can help you plan future lesson plans, classroom speakers, and field trips.

Background Knowledge

This topic is always a great conversation starter! This is my favorite activity to do with my students. The younger the students are, the funnier the responses! This closing circle also gives you insight into the goals and future career aspirations of your older students. It is an activity you do not want to skip!

Procedure

- Pick one stick. This student will begin the circle for the day. Pass the object that you have chosen as your "talking tool" to the person whose craft stick was chosen.

- Begin the closing circle activity by asking the following question: Where do you see yourself in 10 years?

- Give your students a few seconds to think about their answer.

- Ask the student whose stick was chosen to respond first and when finished, pass the "talking tool" to the person on the left or the right. This procedure continues until everyone has a chance to speak.

This closing circle can be used to generate future oral presentations or research projects. For example, ask your students to research different vocations, vehicles, or types of homes in order to have a better idea of what they entail. The possibilities are endless!

Ideas for Your Own Classroom

_____

_____

_____

_____

_____

_____

_____

_____

_____

_____

_____

_____

_____

_____

_____

75. The Story of My Name

Background Knowledge

Ever wonder about the origin of your student's name? Your students will help you with that today! Get ready to hear the story of how your students got their name.

Procedure

- Pick one stick. This student will begin the circle for the day. Pass the object that you have chosen as your "talking tool" to the person whose craft stick was chosen.

- Begin the closing circle activity by asking the following question: Why did your parents choose your name for you?

- Give your students a few seconds to think about their answer.

- Ask the student whose stick was chosen to respond first and when finished, pass the "talking tool" to the person on the left or the right. This procedure continues until everyone has a chance to speak.

Tips and Tricks

There may be some students who do not know the story behind their name. For those students, ask them if they had a hand in helping to name a sibling or a family pet. As an alternative, share the story behind how you got your name or how you went about naming a family member or a pet.

Ideas for Your Own Classroom

76. Nicknames

Goal: Learn the loving names our students receive from their family members and the reason behind those names. This activity causes students to open up to one another and to share personal information about themselves with the class. The more students share with one another, the more comfortable they will feel when working and learning together.

Background Knowledge

Many of us have nicknames that were given to us by our family members. Nicknames can be a shorter version of a name or an entirely different word based on one's personality or a characteristic. Most of the time, they are words of love spoken from parent to child. Students will share these stories today.

Procedure

- Pick one stick. This student will begin the circle for the day. Pass the object that you have chosen as your "talking tool" to the person whose craft stick was chosen.

- Begin the closing circle activity by giving the following prompt: Do you have a nickname? If so, what is it and who calls you that name?

- Give your students a few seconds to think about their answer.

- Ask the student whose stick was chosen to respond first and when finished, pass the "talking tool" to the person on the left or the right. This procedure continues until everyone has a chance to speak.

Tips and Tricks

Teachers often come up with loving nicknames for their students. Have a bank of loving nicknames at your disposal for those students who do not share one at circle time. You can also ask students if they call anyone by a nickname.

Ideas for Your Own Classroom

77. People I Trust

Goal: Discuss the people in your students' lives with whom they can trust. This activity is essential to the health and well-being of students. Much like knowing to call 911 in the event of an emergency, students need to know who they can go to when they are feeling ill, unsafe, or alone.

Background Knowledge

Our students need to name and show appreciation for the people in their lives they trust. These people may include parents, caregivers, bus drivers, supervisors, siblings, teachers, friends, or any person they deem worthy of their trust. This closing circle gives your students the opportunity to talk about the characteristics that make people trustworthy.

Procedure

- Pick one stick. This student will begin the circle for the day. Pass the object that you have chosen as your "talking tool" to the person whose craft stick was chosen.

- Begin the closing circle activity by asking the following questions: Who did you talk to today that you trust? What makes that person trustworthy?

- Give your students a few seconds to think about their answer.

- Ask the student whose stick was chosen to respond first and when finished, pass the "talking tool" to the person on the left or the right. This procedure continues until everyone has a chance to speak.

Tips and Tricks

Look for commonalities among the people your students talk about during this circle. Bring attention to the characteristics that they use to describe what makes someone trustworthy. Challenge students to use these positive characteristics each and every day so they can be trustworthy, too.

Ideas for Your Own Classroom

78. A Cause Close to Your Heart

Goal: Introduce your students to the idea of charity organizations that help others. The benefits of this closing circle are twofold. First, it introduces students to the idea that they can help others that are in need. Second, it can serve as a gateway for students to find help that they might need for themselves, for family members, or for someone in their community.

Background Knowledge

There are many local, national, and international charity groups that inform us about a wide variety of social, political, and spiritual causes. These groups help out people in need around the world. Today's closing circle encourages students to talk about causes they care about while learning about different organizations that help others.

Procedure

- Pick one stick. This student will begin the circle for the day. Pass the object that you have chosen as your "talking tool" to the person whose craft stick was chosen.

- Begin the closing circle activity by asking the following questions: If you had $1,000 to give to a charity, which charity would you give it to and why?

- Give your students a few seconds to think about their answer.

- Ask the student whose stick was chosen to respond first and when finished, pass the "talking tool" to the person on the left or the right. This procedure continues until everyone has a chance to speak.

Ideas for Your Own Classroom

_____

_____

_____

_____

_____

_____

_____

_____

_____

_____

_____

_____

_____

_____

79. Showing Respect to Those Around Us

Goal: Encourage your students to take an active role in showing respect to others. By asking students to reflect upon their actions of the day, this closing circle requires them to think of one thing that they did that was respectful. Focusing their attention on the positive aspects of their day encourages students to continue showing respect when they leave for the day.

Background Knowledge

Many students think that showing respect to others is equivalent to being kind or polite. While this is true, it is not the only way people can show respect. This closing circle explores the many ways we show respect to others on a daily basis.

Procedure

- Pick one stick. This student will begin the circle for the day. Pass the object that you have chosen as your "talking tool" to the person whose craft stick was chosen.

- Begin the closing circle activity by giving the following prompt: Give an example of something you did today to demonstrate respect for someone.

- Give your students a few seconds to think about their answer.

- Ask the student whose stick was chosen to respond first and when finished, pass the "talking tool" to the person on the left or the right. This procedure continues until everyone has a chance to speak.

Tips and Tricks

It is important to let your students know that it does not take a grand gesture to show respect. Demonstrating respect can be as simple as holding a door open for someone, picking something up off of the floor and putting it in the garbage, or saying thank you. Any act of respect, regardless of size or grandeur, shows others you care.

Ideas for Your Own Classroom

80. Family Traditions

Goal: Ask your students to share a tradition they have with their families. This closing circle is a fantastic way to get a peek into the lives of students. This closing circle is especially informative if your students come from multicultural or multireligious backgrounds. The ideas shared in this closing circle will not only provide you with important background information about your students but will also serve as a learning opportunity for your students to see both their similarities and differences.

Background Knowledge

The idea for this closing circle came from one of my students. It was Valentine's Day and he told me that he was excited to eat his lunch because his mom, just like every other Valentine's Day, packed him pink rice to eat. Your students are filled with many heartwarming stories just like this one. This closing circle gives your students a chance to talk about something their family does that makes them feel special.

Procedure

- Pick one stick. This student will begin the circle for the day. Pass the object that you have chosen as your "talking tool" to the person whose craft stick was chosen.

- Begin the closing circle activity by asking the following question: What tradition do you have with your family?

- Give your students a few seconds to think about their answer.

- Ask the student whose stick was chosen to respond first and when finished, pass the "talking tool" to the person on the left or the right. This procedure continues until everyone has a chance to speak.

Ideas for Your Own Classroom

_____

_____

_____

_____

_____

_____

_____

_____

_____

_____

_____

_____

_____

_____

81. How to Be a Good Friend

Goal: Encourage your students to talk about how they are a good friend to others. The more the students feel that they have a positive influence on others, the more likely they are to continue exhibiting that positive behavior. This show of kindness and respect resonates between the students and makes a powerfully positive impact on the classroom dynamic.

Background Knowledge

In order to be a good friend, students need to know how to be a good friend. This includes reminding students about the importance of being kind, honest, and trustworthy. This closing circle gives your students a chance to talk about the wonderful things they do to be a good friend to another.

Procedure

- Pick one stick. This student will begin the circle for the day. Pass the object that you have chosen as your "talking tool" to the person whose craft stick was chosen.

- Begin the closing circle activity by asking the following question: What did you do today to be a good friend?

- Give your students a few seconds to think about their answer.

- Ask the student whose stick was chosen to respond first and when finished, pass the "talking tool" to the person on the left or the right. This procedure continues until everyone has a chance to speak.

Tips and Tricks

Each idea your students bring to this meeting must be acknowledged and appreciated. Congratulate each student for their good acts. This will encourage them to continue to make good choices and treat others with kindness and respect.

Ideas for Your Own Classroom

_____

_____

_____

_____

_____

_____

_____

_____

_____

_____

_____

_____

_____

_____

82. My Responsibilities at School

Goal: Provide an opportunity for your students to discuss the many responsibilities they have while at school each day. This closing circle gives teachers many insights into the home life of their students and also shows students what life is like for others in their class.

Background Knowledge

The biggest responsibility students have at school is to complete assigned work and study. There are, however, other things that students are responsible for doing during the school day. This closing circle gets your students to think about the many responsibilities they undertake while at school.

Procedure

- Pick one stick. This student will begin the circle for the day. Pass the object that you have chosen as your "talking tool" to the person whose craft stick was chosen.

- Begin the closing circle activity by asking the following question: What was one responsible action you did today at school?

- Give your students a few seconds to think about their answer.

- Ask the student whose stick was chosen to respond first and when finished, pass the "talking tool" to the person on the left or the right. This procedure continues until everyone has a chance to speak.

Tips and Tricks

The responsibilities your students undertake while at school vary from day to day. The importance of this closing circle is not the amount of responsible actions your students did during the day, but the fact that they made responsible choices. All responsible actions discussed must be acknowledged and congratulated.

Ideas for Your Own Classroom

_____

_____

_____

_____

_____

_____

_____

_____

_____

_____

_____

_____

_____

_____

83. Hip Hip, Hooray! I Was a Great Person Today!

> **Goal:** Celebrate your students' positive character traits throughout the school day. This closing circle gives your students the opportunity to share kindness and respect by talking nicely about their classmates. The students will leave this closing circle feeling loved and accepted by everyone in the room.

Background Knowledge

In conjunction with the corresponding morning meeting, this closing circle encourages students to talk about their positive character traits that they used during the day.

Procedure

- Pick one stick. This student will begin the circle for the day. Pass the object that you have chosen as your "talking tool" to the person whose craft stick was chosen.

- Begin the closing circle activity by asking the following question: What positive character trait did you try to show today?

- Give your students a few seconds to think about their answer.

- Ask the student whose stick was chosen to respond first and when finished, pass the "talking tool" to the person on the left or the right. This procedure continues until everyone has a chance to speak.

Tips and Tricks

All of our students possess positive character traits but some have a more difficult time showing them during the school day. Some students may be reluctant to share their ideas due to shyness, feelings of embarrassment, or low self-esteem. If this is the case, speak on behalf of the students who are unable to open up. Talk about a positive character trait you see in the students who are unable or unwilling to speak.

Ideas for Your Own Classroom

_____

_____

_____

_____

_____

_____

_____

_____

_____

_____

_____

_____

_____

_____

_____

84. Demonstrate Emotional Control

> **Goal:** Acknowledge that negative emotions occur during the school day but emphasize that showing emotional control in these situations is what is most important. Not all students have the emotional control or know-how to deal with negative emotions. This closing circle will help reemphasize the concepts taught in the coordinating morning meeting to help students reflect upon the tools they can use to control their emotions.

Background Knowledge

Students need practice regulating their negative emotions. In order to do that, they need to acknowledge those emotions and make a conscious effort to control them. This closing circle gives your students a safe place to talk about negative emotions and provides an opportunity to talk about how they changed their mindset.

Procedure

- Pick one stick. This student will begin the circle for the day. Pass the object that you have chosen as your "talking tool" to the person whose craft stick was chosen.

- Begin the closing circle activity by asking the following questions: Which of your negative character traits came out today? How did you try to control it?

- Give your students a few seconds to think about their answer.

- Ask the student whose stick was chosen to respond first and when finished, pass the "talking tool" to the person on the left or the right. This procedure continues until everyone has a chance to speak.

Tips and Tricks

It is important during this closing circle that all students be respectful of each other. Students are taking risks by opening themselves up and it is important that they feel secure when talking in front of the group.

Ideas for Your Own Classroom

_____

_____

_____

_____

_____

_____

_____

_____

_____

_____

_____

_____

85. Give a Little, Take a Little

Goal: Encourage students to reflect on how they were flexible with their teacher or fellow classmates. This activity encourages students to reflect upon their ability to take other people's opinions into account during the school day. It will also give students a chance to talk about how they felt when they chose to be flexible with those around them.

Background Knowledge

Working with others is not always easy. Some students have difficulty allowing others to have a say in group work, while others do very little to contribute to the group. Students need to know that in order for everyone to get what they need and to have success, everyone needs to be flexible. For some that means stepping out of their comfort zone and for others it means settling into the background a little more.

Procedure

- Pick one stick. This student will begin the circle for the day. Pass the object that you have chosen as your "talking tool" to the person whose craft stick was chosen.

- Begin the closing circle activity by giving the following prompt: Give an example of how you were flexible with your teacher or a classmate today.

- Give your students a few seconds to think about their answer.

- Ask the student whose stick was chosen to respond first and when finished, pass the "talking tool" to the person on the left or the right. This procedure continues until everyone has a chance to speak.

Ideas for Your Own Classroom

_____

_____

_____

_____

_____

_____

_____

_____

_____

_____

_____

_____

86. Explain Your Day with an Emoji

Goal: Ask your students to assign an emoji that describes today's school day. Students can use the knowledge they learned from the corresponding morning meeting to help them respond to the prompt. The information gathered from this closing circle will give teachers a firsthand look at how students evaluate their day at school.

Background Knowledge

Emojis are everywhere so why not bring them into the classroom? Students are using these cute little graphics to express their emotions and add a touch of flavor to digital messages. For today's closing circle, ask students to use their emoji knowledge to explain how they felt about their day.

Procedure

- Pick one stick. This student will begin the circle for the day. Pass the object that you have chosen as your "talking tool" to the person whose craft stick was chosen.

- Begin the closing circle activity by giving the following prompt: Assign an emoji to describe your feelings about today.

- Give your students a few seconds to think about their answer.

- Ask the student whose stick was chosen to respond first and when finished, pass the "talking tool" to the person on the left or the right. This procedure continues until everyone has a chance to speak.

Pay careful attention to the children who use negative emojis to talk about their day. For some, verbal expression is difficult, so if a student uses a negative emoji, try to engage in a teacher-student dialogue. If time permits, explore the reasons why they had a bad experience at school today. If you are pressed for time, make a mental note to come back and talk to that child at some point the next day.

Ideas for Your Own Classroom

_____

_____

_____

_____

_____

_____

_____

_____

_____

_____

_____

_____

_____

87. What's Wrong with Being Confident?

Goal: Ask your students to talk about when they feel most confident about themselves. By talking about what makes them confident, students will be returning home with a positive attitude. Teachers can use the information they learn about their students to plan lessons and to build personal relationships with them.

Background Knowledge

Having positive self-esteem takes a lot of work and it does not come naturally to all students. This closing circle gives students a chance to talk about their own self-confidence and the times when they feel at their best both mentally and physically.

Procedure

- Pick one stick. This student will begin the circle for the day. Pass the object that you have chosen as your "talking tool" to the person whose craft stick was chosen.

- Begin the closing circle activity by asking the following question: When do you feel most confident about yourself?

- Give your students a few seconds to think about their answer.

- Ask the student whose stick was chosen to respond first and when finished, pass the "talking tool" to the person on the left or the right. This procedure continues until everyone has a chance to speak.

Tips and Tricks

Most children can tell you what makes them feel self-confident. Some, however, have a harder time. For these children, be prepared to talk about a time when you witnessed their confidence shining through in the classroom. This will boost their self-esteem and send them home with happy hearts.

Ideas for Your Own Classroom

_____

_____

_____

_____

_____

_____

_____

_____

_____

_____

_____

_____

_____

_____

_____

_____

88. Appreciating Teachers

Goal: Ask your students to consider all of the wonderful things their teachers do for them on a daily basis and acknowledge all of the help they provide. While students benefit from talking positively about others, teachers might just get a chance to hear all the wonderful things their students think about them.

Background Knowledge

Teachers do not get enough credit for all the work they do for their students. This closing circle benefits both students and teachers! Students get an opportunity to reflect on all the things their teachers do for them and teachers learn what their students appreciate the most about them.

Procedure

- Pick one stick. This student will begin the circle for the day. Pass the object that you have chosen as your "talking tool" to the person whose craft stick was chosen.

- Begin the closing circle activity by asking the following question: What is one thing a teacher did for you today that you are thankful for?

- Give your students a few seconds to think about their answer.

- Ask the student whose stick was chosen to respond first and when finished, pass the "talking tool" to the person on the left or the right. This procedure continues until everyone has a chance to speak.

Tips and Tricks

If your students talk about you, make sure to thank them for showing their appreciation. Speaking in front of others can be embarrassing for some, and speaking from the heart about a teacher can make that even more difficult. One way to help ease the minds of these students is to reciprocate the appreciation. For each student who talks about you, return the kindness by saying something that they did that made you thankful today.

Ideas for Your Own Classroom

89. Interact with the School Principal

Goal: Encourage students to focus on their positive interactions with the school principal. While students benefit from talking positively about others, some students who do not have a close relationship with the principal will hear the positive comments others have to say. This may encourage some to change their personal mindset about the principal for the better.

Background Knowledge

School principals play a pivotal role in the climate and culture of any school. Besides juggling administrative duties, principals mentor teachers, provide support to students, and work with parents to ensure student success. Today's closing circle gives students an opportunity to reflect on all the things their principal does for the school.

Procedure

- Pick one stick. This student will begin the circle for the day. Pass the object that you have chosen as your "talking tool" to the person whose craft stick was chosen.

- Begin the closing circle activity by providing the following prompt: Tell us about a positive interaction you had with your principal.

- Give your students a few seconds to think about their answer.

- Ask the student whose stick was chosen to respond first and when finished, pass the "talking tool" to the person on the left or the right. This procedure continues until everyone has a chance to speak.

Tips and Tricks

If possible, have your principal participate in this closing circle. If this is not possible, write down the ideas that your students provide. At another time, have the students sign their names on the paper and present it to your principal. Your principal will appreciate the sentiment and the kind words!

Ideas for Your Own Classroom

90. Community Helpers

Goal: Motivate students to acknowledge the importance of community helpers in society. Students will have an opportunity to learn about different community occupations, and it may encourage students to explore career opportunities that provide a service to others.

Background Knowledge

Community helpers play an important role in our lives. We do not truly appreciate all their hard work until, for whatever reason, the service has been disrupted or is unavailable. This closing circle will get students brainstorming about different community helpers and discuss the impact they have on their lives.

Procedure

- Pick one stick. This student will begin the circle for the day. Pass the object that you have chosen as your "talking tool" to the person whose craft stick was chosen.

- Begin the closing circle activity by giving the following prompt: Name a community helper and explain how that person helps you and your family.

- Give your students a few seconds to think about their answer.

- Ask the student whose stick was chosen to respond first and when finished, pass the "talking tool" to the person on the left or the right. This procedure continues until everyone has a chance to speak.

Tips and Tricks

Encourage each student to think of a different community helper. The more ideas students bring to the conversation, the better the discussion!

Ideas for Your Own Classroom

_____

_____

_____

_____

_____

_____

_____

_____

_____

_____

_____

_____

_____

_____

_____

_____

_____

_____

_____

_____

91. Gamers Galore

Goal: Provide an opportunity for students to talk about their favorite board or card game. This activity will provide students with an opportunity to teach others how to do something. This will encourage the students to think carefully about what they want to say and how they want to say it so that everyone understands.

Background Knowledge

With easy access to video games, it is rare that students play board or card games on a regular basis. This closing circle gives students a chance to talk about their favorite games that do not require a television, game console, or access to the Internet.

Procedure

- Pick one stick. This student will begin the circle for the day. Pass the object that you have chosen as your "talking tool" to the person whose craft stick was chosen.

- Begin the closing circle activity by providing the following prompt: Talk about a board or card game that you like to play.

- Give your students a few seconds to think about their answer.

- Ask the student whose stick was chosen to respond first and when finished, pass the "talking tool" to the person on the left or the right. This procedure continues until everyone has a chance to speak.

Tips and Tricks

Remind students that this closing circle is about game titles and not about how to play the game. Since time is limited, stress the importance of being concise when talking about the game of their choice. If students are really excited about the topic, think about planning a board or card game club or period. These games not only require skill, but also enforce taking turns, strategizing, and maintaining emotional control.

Ideas for Your Own Classroom

92. Thinking of Others Before Ourselves

Goal: Motivate students to think about how they put the needs of others ahead of their own. This social skill is important, as being able to put the needs of someone else before our own is essential when maintaining relationships with others.

Background Knowledge

One of the earliest lessons children learn in school is to share and be kind to others. As students grow and mature, they begin to show that they are capable of interpreting the emotions and needs of others. This closing circle gives students an opportunity to share the ways in which they have put their needs or wants aside in order to help others.

Procedure

- Pick one stick. This student will begin the circle for the day. Pass the object that you have chosen as your "talking tool" to the person whose craft stick was chosen.

- Begin the closing circle activity by providing the following prompt: Talk about a time when you put someone else's needs above your own.

- Give your students a few seconds to think about their answer.

- Ask the student whose stick was chosen to respond first and when finished, pass the "talking tool" to the person on the left or the right. This procedure continues until everyone has a chance to speak.

This closing circle is not limited to discussions about family, friends, or even strangers. Many students are responsible for taking care of family pets and at times, pet caretakers have to put their needs aside for the sake of their animals.

Ideas for Your Own Classroom

_____

_____

_____

_____

_____

_____

_____

_____

_____

_____

_____

_____

_____

_____

_____

_____

_____

93. Lending a Helping Hand at Home

Goal: Challenge students to think about what they can do to help their family members when they go home. This allows students a chance to set a plan in place to do something to help their families. This also gives them a chance to show their families how responsible they can be.

Background Knowledge

This closing circle challenges students to think about what they can do to help their family when they return home. Thinking about it now increases the chances of the students actually following through with it when they get home!

Procedure

- Pick one stick. This student will begin the circle for the day. Pass the object that you have chosen as your "talking tool" to the person whose craft stick was chosen.

- Begin the closing circle activity by asking the following question: What is one thing you can do tonight to help out your family?

- Give your students a few seconds to think about their answer.

- Ask the student whose stick was chosen to respond first and when finished, pass the "talking tool" to the person on the left or the right. This procedure continues until everyone has a chance to speak.

Tips and Tricks

Try to get students to think outside of the box when it comes to things that they can do to help their families. It might be as simple as completing their homework without complaining. Whatever your students choose to do, make sure to bring a lot of excitement to their ideas. The important part of this circle is that the students are developing a plan that encourages them to think of others.

Ideas for Your Own Classroom

94. This Classroom Smells So Good!

Goal: Help students connect a smell they associate with their classroom to an emotion. By doing this, students will be exploring how the outside world around them contributes to their positive well-being, and they will be able to share their emotions in a safe environment.

Background Knowledge

One day, a colleague of mine was applying lip gloss while in the classroom and her student said, "You smell like kindergarten." At that moment I realized how certain classroom aromas are attached to positive, heart-warming memories in our students. This closing circle taps into the positive memories that each student has thanks to the everyday smells of our classrooms.

Procedure

- Pick one stick. This student will begin the circle for the day. Pass the object that you have chosen as your "talking tool" to the person whose craft stick was chosen.

- Begin the closing circle activity by asking the following questions: What is a smell you associate with your school or classroom? What emotion do you associate with that smell?

- Give your students a few seconds to think about their answer.

- Ask the student whose stick was chosen to respond first and when finished, pass the "talking tool" to the person on the left or the right. This procedure continues until everyone has a chance to speak.

Ideas for Your Own Classroom

_____

_____

_____

_____

_____

_____

_____

_____

_____

_____

_____

_____

_____

95. Would You Rather...?

Goal: Dare your students to contemplate and choose one not-so-great thing over another. This closing circle will encourage your students to use their critical thinking skills and prepare arguments to support their point of view.

Background Knowledge

"Would You Rather" questions are great conversation starters. Most "Would You Rather" questions require choosing between two or more unpleasant options. This specific closing circle does not present anything unpleasant. Instead, it makes students think carefully about their choice and their rationale for choosing it.

Procedure

- Pick one stick. This student will begin the circle for the day. Pass the object that you have chosen as your "talking tool" to the person whose craft stick was chosen.

- Begin the closing circle activity by asking the following question: Would you rather keep the timeline of your school the way it is or go to school longer each day to finish the year earlier?

- Give your students a few seconds to think about their answer.

- Ask the student whose stick was chosen to respond first and when finished, pass the "talking tool" to the person on the left or the right. This procedure continues until everyone has a chance to speak.

Tips and Tricks

A change in the school schedule has both positive and negative implications on society. This closing circle offers a glimpse into how students take other people's lives and timetables into consideration. It is important to get students to think outside of their own needs in this situation, as a change in the school schedule can implicate an entire community.

Ideas for Your Own Classroom

96. What Do I Need Math For?

> **Goal:** Expose students to the various parts of our lives that use mathematics. Many students do not realize the impact that mathematics have on our everyday lives. This closing circle will introduce students to various life skills and occupations where mathematics play an integral role.

Background Knowledge

Many students struggle with mathematics. Because of this struggle, many students experience anxiety and wish they could just quit math! Many believe they do not need math for their futures. This closing circle exposes students to how we use math in our daily lives, and how their career paths will most likely include some element of mathematics.

Procedure

- Pick one stick. This student will begin the circle for the day. Pass the object that you have chosen as your "talking tool" to the person whose craft stick was chosen.

- Begin the closing circle activity by asking the following question: Besides using math at school, where else do we use math?

- Give your students a few seconds to think about their answer.

- Ask the student whose stick was chosen to respond first and when finished, pass the "talking tool" to the person on the left or the right. This procedure continues until everyone has a chance to speak.

Tips and Tricks

Use this time to add information about occupations that use some element and knowledge of math. Also, give examples of how we use math every day. Some students might not realize just how much they use, and rely on mathematics, in their daily lives.

Ideas for Your Own Classroom

_____

_____

_____

_____

_____

_____

_____

_____

_____

_____

_____

_____

_____

_____

_____

_____

97. I Cannot Live Without...

Goal: Discover who or what students value at this point in their lives. Knowing this kind of information about your students will help you form stronger emotional bonds with them, and you will be able to work their responses into educational activities throughout the school year.

Background Knowledge

This closing circle provides great insight into what your students hold near and dear to them. Depending on the age and maturity level of each student, their responses may shock or even surprise you. Regardless, this information will prove to be valuable when looking for ways to strengthen your relationship with all your students.

Procedure

- Pick one stick. This student will begin the circle for the day. Pass the object that you have chosen as your "talking tool" to the person whose craft stick was chosen.

- Begin the closing circle activity by giving the following prompts: If I didn't have _____ in my life, I wouldn't know what to do.

- Give your students a few seconds to think about their answer.

- Ask the student whose stick was chosen to respond first and when finished, pass the "talking tool" to the person on the left or the right. This procedure continues until everyone has a chance to speak.

Tips and Tricks

If your students are providing mostly answers with material items or common conveniences they would miss, ask them to think about people or pets that they would have a hard time living without. Directing the discussion toward people and animals will make this closing circle more personal, emotional, and memorable.

Ideas for Your Own Classroom

_____

_____

_____

_____

_____

_____

_____

_____

_____

_____

_____

_____

_____

_____

_____

98. Celebrate the Small Stuff

Goal: Consider and acknowledge any areas of improvement made since the beginning of the school year. Students need a chance to feel proud of their accomplishments, no matter how big or small they are. This circle will also give all students a chance to feel special and important in front of their peers.

Background Knowledge

Much like parents who don't "see" their children grow, teachers often do not realize how much their students learn and improve during the school year. This closing circle gives both you and the students insight into just how far you have all come in a short period of time.

Procedure

- Pick one stick. This student will begin the circle for the day. Pass the object that you have chosen as your "talking tool" to the person whose craft stick was chosen.

- Begin the closing circle activity by asking the following question: What is one thing you couldn't do earlier this year that you can do now?

- Give your students a few seconds to think about their answer.

- Ask the student whose stick was chosen to respond first and when finished, pass the "talking tool" to the person on the left or the right. This procedure continues until everyone has a chance to speak.

Ideas for Your Own Classroom

_____

_____

_____

_____

_____

_____

_____

_____

_____

_____

_____

_____

_____

_____

_____

99. Random Acts of Kindness

Goal: Encourage your students to think about doing random acts of kindness on a daily basis. This closing circle will give students a chance to talk about something nice they did for someone else. Because of this discussion, students will have several examples of acts of kindness they can do for others.

Background Knowledge

Random acts of kindness can be completed anytime, anywhere, for anyone, and at no cost. Students need to practice being kind to others and accepting kindness from others. This closing circle increases awareness about the need for kindness and congratulates students for acting in benevolent ways. You can also use this time to encourage students to do something nice for others every day.

Procedure

- Pick one stick. This student will begin the circle for the day. Pass the object that you have chosen as your "talking tool" to the person whose craft stick was chosen.

- Begin the closing circle activity by asking the following question: What is one random act of kindness that you did for someone today?

- Give your students a few seconds to think about their answer.

- Ask the student whose stick was chosen to respond first and when finished, pass the "talking tool" to the person on the left or the right. This procedure continues until everyone has a chance to speak.

Tips and Tricks

Let students know that random acts of kindness do not need to be extravagant. Being kind can be as simple as holding the door open for someone, helping someone pick up something that fell on the floor, or complimenting someone on getting a good grade. Sometimes just giving someone a high five is enough to make a person's day!

Ideas for Your Own Classroom

_____

_____

_____

_____

_____

_____

_____

_____

_____

_____

_____

_____

_____

_____

100. Up for Grabs

Goal: Your students will show their confidence by choosing what they want to contribute to the closing circle. This closing circle encourages students to exercise their leadership skills by suggesting a topic and leading the circle for everyone.

Background Knowledge

After 50 morning meetings and 49 closing circles, your students are now familiar with how they are run. It is now time to let the students take control over what they want to say at this circle. It is their time to shine!

Procedure

- Pick one stick. This student will begin the circle for the day. Pass the object that you have chosen as your "talking tool" to the person whose craft stick was chosen.

- Begin the closing circle activity by asking the following prompt: What would you like to say at today's closing circle?

- Give your students a few seconds to think about their answer.

- Ask the student whose stick was chosen to respond first and when finished, pass the "talking tool" to the person on the left or the right. This procedure continues until everyone has a chance to speak.

Tips and Tricks

For this final activity, take a step back and let the students run the entire closing circle. This is your opportunity to watch and enjoy all the progress you and your students accomplished during the morning meetings and closing circles! Marvel in the improvements your students made and the sense of community that has grown among all the members of the classroom.

Ideas for Your Own Classroom

Conclusion

Congratulations! You have successfully completed 100 activities that strengthened the bond between you and your students. You witnessed your students fine-tune interpersonal skills that will stay with them for the rest of their lives. You provided a toolbox of strategies to help them through their anger and frustrations. And, most importantly, you opened your students up to a whole new way of thinking and interacting with others. And did I mention that you were able to do all of that, and more, in only 20 minutes a day? Way to go!

Morning meetings and closing circles have become a staple of my daily classroom routine and I suspect they are now a part of yours, as well. Every new meeting or circle provides us with another opportunity to learn about our students. Whether it be about their home lives, their hopes and dreams, or even their insecurities, these mini get-togethers bring out the best in our students. Doesn't your heart burst with pride every time you see your students use a tip or strategy discussed at a meeting or circle? Of course you do! Relish that pride because you have earned it. Without your leadership and gentle guidance throughout the process, your students would not be where they are today.

This book may be finished but it is just your beginning! I challenge you to continue creating your own morning meetings and closing circles. If you are struggling for ideas, look no further than your own classroom. Look for triumphs, tribulations, positive and negative attitudes, and curriculum content that needs to be revised. Add an element of current events. Introduce your students to debating. Surf the Internet for easy-to-implement games and tasks that require teamwork. Better yet, have your students come up with a list of their own ideas. Now that they are familiar with how morning meetings and closing circles are run in your classroom, let the students lead the development and implementation of the next 100!

With you leading the way, your students will continue to gain confidence in themselves. They will continue to be more mindful of others. They will continue making positive strides inside and outside of the classroom. As for you, you will continue to grow and strengthen your bond with each of your students and marvel in the sense of community you helped to create and maintain in your classroom.

I applaud you!

Bibliography

Anderson, Tiffany Chane'l. *Closing the Achievement Gap: Reaching and Teaching High Poverty Learners: 101 Top Strategies to Help High Poverty Learners Succeed*. New York: iUniverse, 2007.

Correa-Connolly, Melissa. *99 Activities and Greetings: Great for Morning Meeting—and Other Meetings, Too!* Turners Falls, MA: Northeast Foundation for Children, 2004.

Davis, Carol. *80 Morning Meeting Ideas for Grades 3–6*. Turners Falls, MA: Center for Responsive Schools, Inc., 2017.

Durden, Felicia. *Morning Meetings for Special Education Classrooms: 101 Fun Ideas, Creative Activities and Adaptable Techniques*. New York: Ulysses Press, 2017.

Januszka, Dana, and Kristen Vincent. *Closing Circles: 50 Activities for Ending the Day in a Positive Way*. Turners Falls, MA: Northeast Foundation for Children, Inc., 2012.

Kriete, Roxann, and Carol Davis. *The Morning Meeting Book: K-8*. Turners Falls, MA: Northeast Foundation for Children, 2017.

Lally, Phillipa, Cornelia H. M. Van Jaarsveld, Henry W. W. Potts, and Jane Wardle. "How Are Habits Formed: Modelling Habit Formation in the Real World." *European Journal of Social Psychology* 40, no. 6 (2010): 998–1009. https://doi.org/10.1002/ejsp.674.

Roser, Susan Lattanzi. *80 Morning Meeting Ideas: for Grades K-2*. Turners Falls, MA: Center for Responsive Schools, Inc., 2016.

Styles, Donna. *Class Meetings: Building Leadership, Problem-Solving and Decision-Making Skills in the Respectful Classroom*. Ontario, Canada: Pembroke Publishers, 2001.

Vance, Emily. *Class Meetings: Young Children Solving Problems Together*. Washington, DC: National Association for the Education of Young Children, 2014.

Whyte, Donna. *Morning Meeting, Afternoon Wrap-up: How to Motivate Kids, Teach to Their Strengths, and Meet Your State's Standards*. Washington, DC: Crystal Springs Books, 2004.

Acknowledgments

To Ulysses Press and their wonderful team. You took a leap of faith when you contacted me to write this book. You cannot imagine the honor and privilege it has been for me to be a part of this project. Because of your belief in me and my ideas, you have allowed me to fulfill my dream of becoming a published author. I will be forever grateful for this opportunity.

To Claire Sielaff, thank you so much for encouraging me to begin this new literary adventure. The kindness you showed me at the beginning of this project is appreciated more than you will ever know. Without you, I would never have had the confidence to attempt this writing adventure. You patiently answered my many questions and guided me through the pre-writing process, and as a new author, your support was essential and a true gift.

To Renee Rutledge, I thank my lucky stars that you were assigned to be my project manager and editor. Your keen eye, attention to detail, and ability to keep me on track was a true gift. Every correction, every suggestion, and every email sent was exactly what I needed to hear and what my words needed in order to make this book become a reality. You took a new author, guided her from beginning to end, and helped her accomplish one of her life's goals. There are not enough thank-yous in the world to express how grateful I am to you and all the effort you made to help me make my dream come true.

To Linda Déragon, your enthusiasm upon learning about this book was through the roof from the moment I told you about it. Your positive energy and excitement kept me motivated until the end. Thank you very much for allowing me to bounce ideas off of you and giving me constructive feedback when I asked for it.